I0416273

LABOUR CONTROL IN BELIZE, JAMAICA AND THE UNITED STATES OF AMERICA

The History Dissertation Prizewinner

Lulu Press Incorporated

Peter Hitchen at LULU Publishing

Education and Multi-Cultural Cohesion in the Caribbean: the Case of Belize, 1931 – 1981

Key Issues in the American Saga: the Quest for Freedom

Labour Control in Belize, Jamaica and United States. The History Dissertation Prizewinner.

Key Issues in History: An English Social History Reader

All the above available for print order or digital download from the publisher below:

http://www.lulu.com/phitchen8

and at

http://www.freewebs.com/multiculturalism/

LABOUR CONTROL IN BELIZE, JAMAICA AND THE UNITED STATES OF AMERICA
The History Dissertation Prizewinner

Peter Hitchen

Published by LULU Press Incorporated.

Distributed in the USA by LULU Printing Services Ltd.

Labour Control in Belize, Jamaica and the United States of America

Copyright © Peter Hitchen 2005

The right of Peter Hitchen to be identified as the author of this work has been asserted by him in accordance with the Copyright, Designs and Patents Act 1988.

Published by LULU Press Incorporated.

Distributed in the USA by LULU Printing Services Ltd.

ISBN: 1- 4116-5715-2

1st Published 2005

Essay first delivered 1994.

Typeset in Times New Roman

All rights reserved. No part of this publication may be reproduced, stored in a retrieval system or transmitted, in any form or by any means without the prior permission in writing of the author, or as expressly permitted by law, or under the terms agreed with the appropriate reprographics rights organisation. Enquiries concerning reproduction outside the above should also be addressed to the author at the address above.
You must not circulate this book in any binding or cover and you must impose this same condition on any acquirer

www.lulu.com

Printed in the USA by LULU Printing Services Ltd.

Peter Hitchen

For Mum

Review

This is a dissertation by Dr. Peter Hitchen, Professor of North American history in the Department of Humanities at the University of Central Lancashire. It examines the role of slavery as utilized in the mahogany harvest of Belize (British Honduras) and the sugar plantations of Jamaica, both dating from 1830, and the plantation system of the southern United States. Inherent in Hitchen's dissertation is reaffirmation of the golden rule: "He who has the gold, makes the rules," for it is demonstrated that neither an act of Parliament nor a Civil War could change the fundamental economics of the slavery system. Those who retained power, whether through property ownership, wealth, education, or other form of control, dictated the labour control system. Slaves, although freed, remained dependent upon the power holders for their very survival so were free in name only. They continued as indentured servants long after being granted their "freedom."

Dr. Hitchen's dissertation is flawless, from his presentation to his footnotes to his extensive bibliography. It should be required reading for anyone studying the issue of slavery. It is rated a five in all categories. But more significant than this reviewer's comments are those of the following peers, experts in the area of study undertaken by Dr. Hitchen: "The highest rated dissertation. Admired for its ambition, soundness, sophistication, and key concepts. No more to add, except, well done." Dr. Keith Vernon and Dr. John Manley, University of Central Lancashire.

Review by Steven M. Ulmen, www.gloomwing.com

Peter Hitchen

Labour Control in Belize, Jamaica and the United States of America

Author

Peter Hitchen received his Doctorate in February 2003 and teaches North American history at the Department of Humanities, University of Central Lancashire. His main area of expertise is the Caribbean State–Church education system, but he also has research interests in comparative (United States, British and Caribbean) history of education particularly aspects of impecunious funding for African Caribbean/American schools. He has published or accepted for publication articles and  books with *History of Education, History of Education Researcher*. He is currently adapting his oral history database for book length publication.

He lives with his beloved wife, three of four grown-up children, one of two grandchildren and the incredible 'Basher' (German Shepherd) in Cleveleys on the Northwest coast of England.

Cover design LULU Printing services.

Peter Hitchen

CONTENTS

Labour Control in Belize, Jamaica and the United States of America

Abstract

This dissertation focuses on Post-Emancipation systems of labour control using a comparative analysis of the United States, from 1865 to the 'Redemption' in 1877, and the British Caribbean colonies of Belize and Jamaica, from final Emancipation in 1838 until the establishment of Crown Colony rule, in 1871 for Belize, and 1366 for Jamaica. The purpose of the comparison being to highlight the differences and similarities to further an understanding of why certain historical phenomena occurred in one or two regions and not in another.

The fundamental argument being that there was no simple step from slavery to freedom; that the local oligarchies in each region attempted to prevent, with varying degrees of success, the former Negro slave from attaining full freedom, economically or politically, after Emancipation. The paper tackles the extent to which they were prepared to go with coercive tactics to achieve their aims.

The chapters develop and prove the argument using a variety of secondary sources to identify current historiographical research. Extensive use of primary materials, such as government reports, other official documents and correspondence, newspapers and oral testimony, will uphold the overall and supporting arguments.

Peter Hitchen

Acknowledgements

Many thanks are due to the staff of the University of central Lancashire Library, particularly those involved in inter-library loans; who managed to procure seemingly endless requests during last summer. Some of these were invaluable primary materials, which saved me an expensive trip to the Public Record Office.

Special thanks are due to my supervisor, John Manley, without whose constant attention this dissertation would not have gathered in quite so organised a fashion. Further to Keith Vernon whose patience and assistance helped clear the way and minimise the tumult of progression, and a myriad of other pastoral details.

I see from most acknowledgements that historians invariably thank their spouses. I now understand why. Heather is a second year undergraduate, and we have three children at primary school. Yet she still managed to ensure that this third year 'Dissertationist' was given the 'lion's share' of space and time in her already busy schedule.

Whatever shape this paper is now in, the remaining faults rest entirely with me.

P.R.H. 3 May 1994.

Glossary of terms

1. DIALECTIC: The notion, developed by Marx and advanced by Engels, expresses the view that development depends on the clash of contradictions, and the creation of a new, more advanced synthesis out of these clashes. The dialectical process involves the three moments: thesis, antithesis, and synthesis. Less abstract, the key to the dialectic, as I understand it, is the 'relational' character of reality, or as Engels put it in *Dialectics of Nature*, dialectic is the 'science of universal inter-connection.' Human reality cannot be validly examined without an examination of its relations to its environment and the process of change.

2. ELITE: This refers to a minority group, which has the power or influence over others, and is recognised as in some way superior. Unlike class, elite power may not rest on economic position and power, but on that section of the dominant class with political power.

3. HEGEMONY: A term used by Antonio Gramsci concerning the domination of one class over others by a combination of political and ideological means. Hegemonies attempt to maintain a balance between coercion and consent, varying from society to society but with the emphasis on consent.

4. LATIFUNDIA: A large agrarian estate in which the labourer is subject to the authoritative control, normally though not exclusively, of an absent patron.

5. MAYA: The Maya are possibly the most celebrated of the classical civilizations of Mesoamerica. Originating in the Yucatan approximately 2600 B.C., they rose to prominence about A.D. 250 in contemporary southern Mexico, Guatemala, western Honduras, El Salvador, and Belize. Although Belize is at the centre of the former Mayan Empire, the current Mayan descendents predominantly came from Mexico and Guatemala. Most of the initial Mayans fell victim to plagues or armed conflict. Presently, three groups are represented, the Yucatec Maya from Yucatan Mexico, the Mopan from the

Peten, Guatemala, and the Kekchi who migrated from the Verapaz region of Guatemala. In the southern Toledo district of Belize, where the Kekchi and Mopan dwell, they together comprise the largest percentage of Mayan descendents in Belize today and have remained the most traditional and culturally distinct.

6. OLIGARCHY: One of Aristotle's basic forms of government, the rule of a few, in their own interests.

7. PATERNALISM: The use of a term describing the relationship between a Father and a child to characterise that between superiors and subordinates, a system of dependency with ideological dimensions, emphasising the caring role and dealing with the whole person. It does not separate work and non-work life, and assumes an inequality of power.

8. PLANTATION: As for 'Latifundia' but the estate is usually given over to mono crop production.

9. PLANTERS: Owners or operators of the above, in the New World, the dominant economic and political group before Emancipation

The slave went free; stood for a brief moment in the sun, then moved back again toward slavery.

W. E. B Dubois, *Black Reconstruction.*

Caribbean and South in physical context

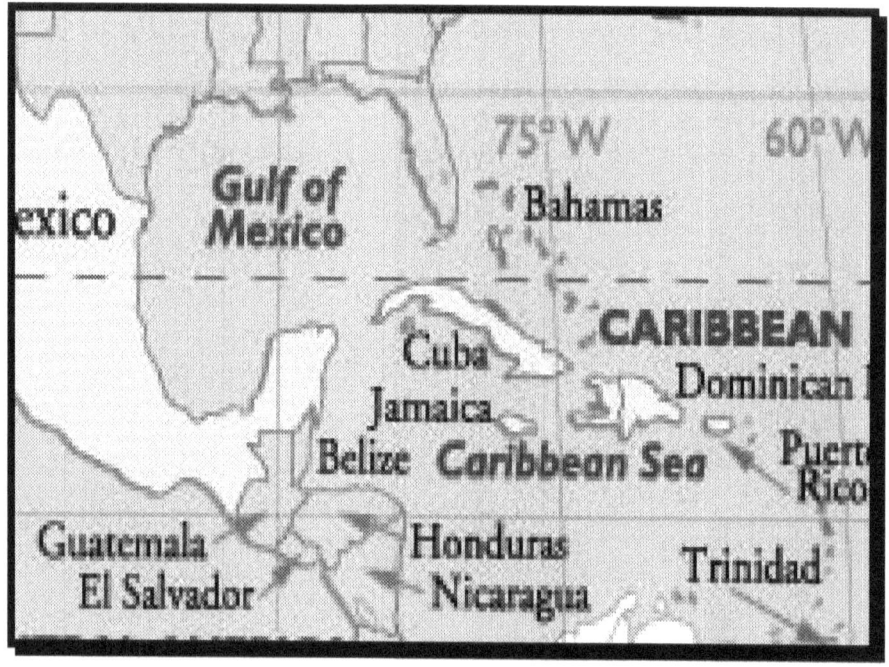

Peter Hitchen

Introduction

The overall contention of this dissertation is that the antinomy of slavery and freedom, in relation to the post-Emancipation period, of the British West Indies and the United States South needs to be abandoned. Freedom was merely a legal status in 1838 and 1865 respectively. Ex-slaves were never freed from the constraints of persistent power structures; thus it is argued that Negroes in both the Caribbean and the South were returned to a position of involuntary servitude as rapidly as possible by the master-class. While this paper will present evidence to show changes in the composition of this class, the focus is predominantly on the planters and foresters as groups, who were the masters before Emancipation, and their struggle to maintain their hegemony.

Consideration was given, in selecting each area not simply to their similarities as former slave holding communities, but to a sufficient degree of differences to justify meaningful comparison. Ability to maintain control of the

Labour Control in Belize, Jamaica and the United States of America

society in general was different in each case, although all three began to abandon ideological methods of paternalism in favour of legal and economic controls quite early. Belize gives a clear, unambiguous example of strong control with minimal resistance, and provides a useful measure to set against the inadequacies of the other systems: For instance, the Jamaican planter's inability to monopolize all land, or the South's political impotence.

The periods under discussion approximate to major turning points in the political and economic life of each community; 1865 and 1838 being the beginning of full Emancipation in the South and British Caribbean respectively. The year 1877 represents the complete acquisition of political control in the South, with the consequent re-enactment of many racially biased laws. In Jamaica, 1866 and Belize, 1871 represent the de jure surrender of political control to the British Crown, although the local ruling class continued to rule as unelected councils rather than elected assemblies.

In addressing the overall argument, Chapter 1 will provide a relevant analytical overview of each society. Just how the former masters attempted to retain control over their workforce will be discussed in the remaining chapters, beginning in Chapter 2 with the question of economic independence and land control as fundamental to the extent of all further controls. In relation to this, Chapters 3 and 4 will illustrate how the elites maintained that dominance with the law, a system of one-sided contracts, debt servitude, and violence. This final point will be discussed at length in Chapter 4 to reveal that all the other systems of control require violent action to underpin them, and local oligarchies, as distinct from political rulers, will resort to whatever level of violence they deem necessary to maintain their control, even if this requires crossing the legal line. Each area provides contrasting evidence for this argument.

The conclusion of this dissertation will summarise the supporting arguments in relation to the overall argument. Then briefly examine the subject

Peter Hitchen

of labour control as part of the wider issue of social control with suggestions for further research.

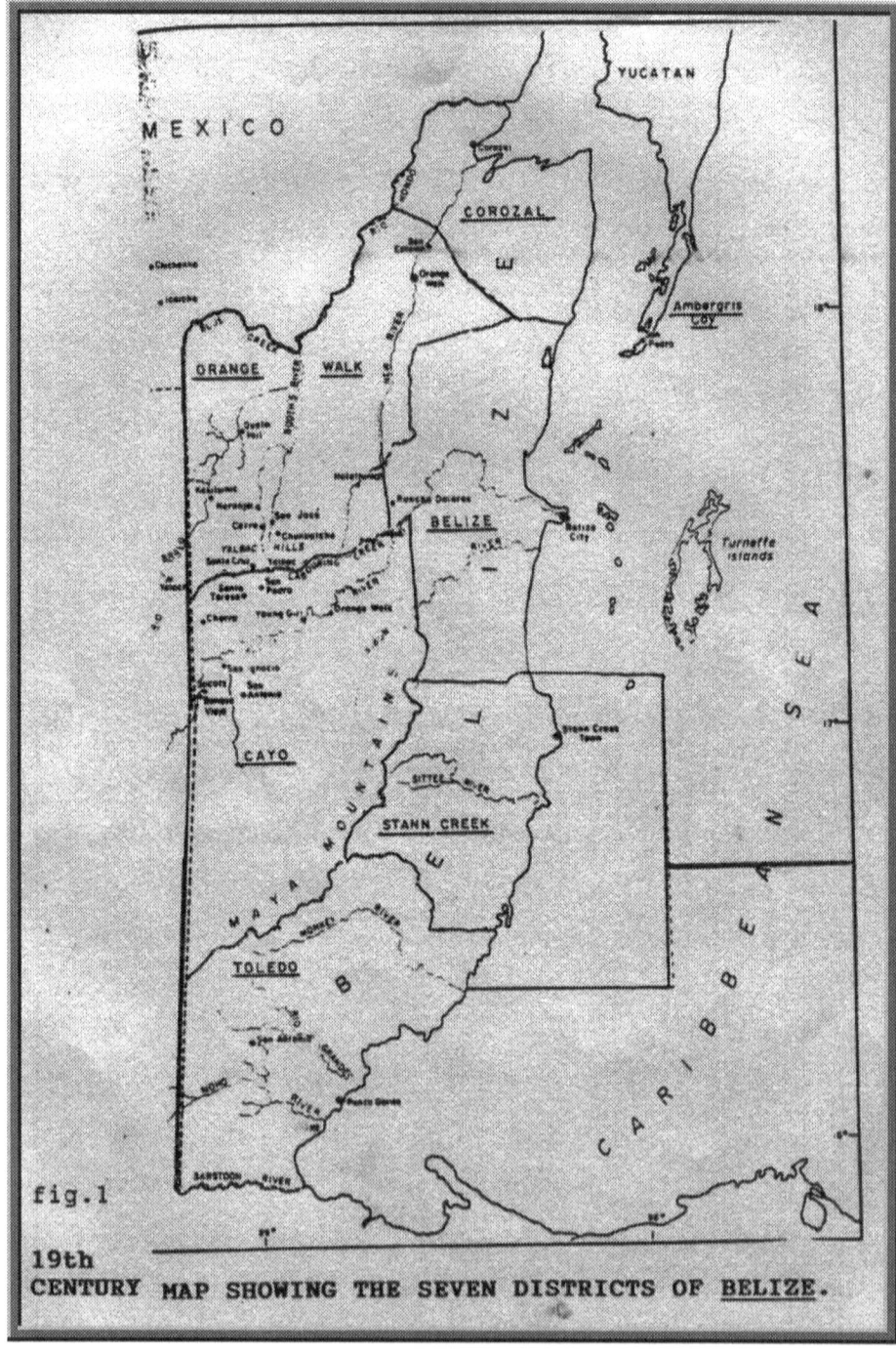

fig.1

19th
CENTURY MAP SHOWING THE SEVEN DISTRICTS OF BELIZE.

1
The Economic Situation

In order to comprehend the various methods that were applied in the transfer from one system of labour control to another, it is necessary to provide some assessment of the economic circumstances in each of the regions under examination. In this section and for the purpose of clarity, Belize, Jamaica and the United States South (South) will be dealt with separately, with closer comparisons in subsequent chapters. Finally, this chapter will draw some conclusions on the differences and similarities between these areas.

Belize 1830-1871

Known to the British Government as 'British Honduras', the settlement was known locally as Belize and with this in mind, the paper shall throughout use the term Belize.

Belize has been described as a Plantation/Latifundia society, [1] sharing characteristics with other societies in the West Indies. Namely: Land monopoly, resulting in dispossessed labourers becoming dependent upon the landowners for work, and large areas of productive land lying idle .and waiting for labour to be spared from the main work production. [2]

Colonial societies are not 'autonomous social realities' but are subject to changes in demand from the metropolis. [3] Belize, with a population in 1838 of fewer than three thousand, or one person per two-square miles, was from its earliest settlement in the seventeenth-century, 'A single product dominated society'. [4] After the development of synthetic dyes logwood extraction shifted from coastal logging to the more expensive and labour intensive mahogany cutting, which then controlled the Belizean economy from the 1770s to the 1950s. By the mid-19th century due to the increased costs of going further inland for mahogany, and a fall in demand with prices going from 5d per square foot in 1847 to 2d in 1868, most of the land became concentrated in the hands of London based companies such as the Belize Estate and Produce Company. [5]

Mahogany foresters

Labour Control in Belize, Jamaica and the United States of America

Meeting the metropolitan market's demands meant that agriculture was neglected and much fresh produce had to be imported, resulting in the chronic under use of land. As Green says succinctly:

> There was no agricultural tradition in Belize, no staple product of the soil, no peasantry. The land was held by a few settlers who controlled all the domestic trade or otherwise, and ran the political and administrative machinery of the settlement. [6]

Clearly, Belize was a business venture that the settlers were not going to sacrifice once a comparatively large and free population emerged between 1834 and 1838.

Although the Belizean economy at the time of Emancipation was similar to Jamaica, the effects of change in British demands were delayed in

Exports of Mahogany from Belize, 1830-1846; 1857-1868			
Date	Mahogany in 1,000 superficial feet	Date	Mahogany in 1,000 superficial feet
1830	4,557	1857	7,267 ★
1831	3,866	1858	6,275
1832	5,015	1859	5,436
1833	4,565	1860	8,090
1834	6,308	1861	8,057
1835	6,421	1862	8,885
1836	9,768	1863	6,196
1837	8,500	1864	7,135
1838-44	.....	1865	5,240
1845	9,320	1866	5,167
1846	13,719 ★	1867	4,156
1847-56	.....	1868	3,007

Table shows the rise in the mahogany trade and subsequent decline from 1856.

Belize due to the boom in mahogany trade, which saw a peak of fourteen million feet in 1846. Nevertheless, from then a slump in demand brought on by

Peter Hitchen

a glut in British mahogany stocks, and a change in ship manufacture from wood to iron, created a situation of chronic unemployment still visible today. [7]

However, mahogany remained the dominant product until the mid-twentieth century, but fluctuations in orders had a pervasive effect upon the whole colony. As Gibbs says,

> When London and Liverpool prices current showed an advance there were cheerful smiling faces in the counting houses and bustle and activity around the wharves; when prices fell there was a dullness everywhere; lounging woodcutters on the bridge, instead of being away in the woods axe in hand. [8.]

The state of the mahogany trade is important for this paper because it was the 'chief determinant for labour'.[9] The 'boom' explains the masters' desire to retain a strict control over a workforce they had always considered to be numerically inadequate. The depression loosened the demand for labour, but little alternative employment was available. In spite of some attempts at farm development Belize has consistently suffered, under colonial rule from severe unemployment problem, not totally eradicated beyond Independence in 1981.

Jamaica 1830-1866

Similarly, Jamaica was a Plantation/Latifundia society, though here known as estates. Fortunately, more information is available regarding Jamaican estates than for forestlands, for the National Library of Jamaica holds a collection of approximately twenty thousand plans of urban and rural landholdings.[10]

As in Belize, the Jamaican economy was dominated, from about 1730, by the single crop of sugar, becoming the major producer for the British Empire. Crop production accounted for half of the 311,000 total slave population before Emancipation, [11] but not including other plantation workers such as house servants.

Unfortunately, labour relations were troublesome from the outset. In 1831 a serious slave rebellion was prompted by the perception that the King

Labour Control in Belize, Jamaica and the United States of America

had granted freedom but the planters had conspired to its withholding. Peace was eventually restored in February of 1832, and while only twelve whites died several hundred Blacks were killed with property valued at £1,500,000 destroyed. Many Blacks were flogged to death, one in Montego Bay after five hundred lashes. [12] The rebellion is significant for its effect on the minority white population's behaviour after Emancipation as they became determined not to allow political freedoms to Blacks.

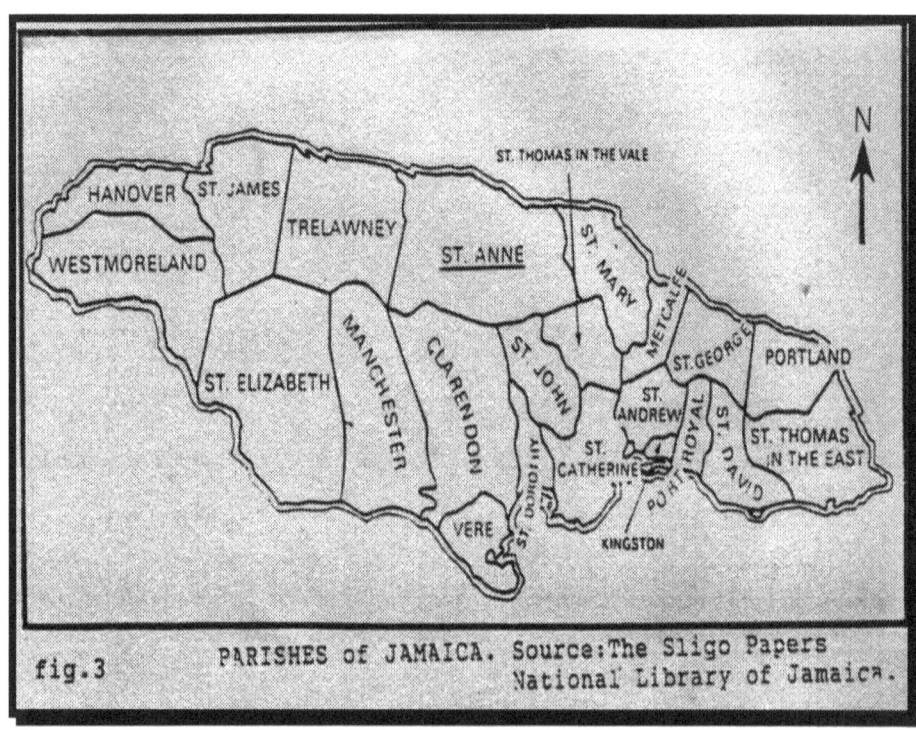

fig.3   PARISHES of JAMAICA. Source:The Sligo Papers National Library of Jamaica.

Slavery ended in the British Empire on 1 August 1834, with final Emancipation a further four years after this interim apprenticeship period. The British Government dispensed £20,000,000 in compensation, but most of Jamaica's share went in paying off creditors in London leaving little for local investment or wage paying. Green argues that Britain, being ruled by a propertied class, could hardly avoid the issue of compensation. An Act of Parliament confiscating millions of pounds worth of property would set a dangerous precedent in English law.[13]

In the interim, apprenticeship was seen by the British Government as a failure.[14] Supposedly a period of transition from slavery to wage labour, it was used in Belize and Jamaica as an extension of slavery. However, under this system Blacks were only obliged to work without payment for forty and a half hours each week. At other times the system 'enabled ex-slaves some small accumulation of wealth' by the growing and selling of their produce at 'regular Sunday markets'.[15] Thus allowing many to buy what spare land the planters could not control, and abandon the estates in favour of subsistence farming.

Therefore, movement-minimisation was important to Jamaican planters controlling estates as large as 7,000 acres with the mean average at 1,000 acres. The mean average Black worker population was 223, though this ranged as high as 600. Thirty-six per-cent of estates had 200 or more Black workers. This compares with five per-cent on the Louisiana sugar plantations. The 19th century began with an all time peak for Jamaican sugar production, of 100,000 tons exported in 1805, plummeting to 5,000 tons by the end of a century long decline.[16]

The South's fears regarding the Emancipation of its slaves by the North were based on a perceived example of decline in the West Indies. Wilkins gives the following account,

> The West Indies are hastening with a very quick step towards ruin accounts of widespread disturbance throughout the West Indies were reported in South Carolina--and the loss of property by the apprentices refusal to work was as 'ruinous and as much to be dreaded as the torch of the firebrand or the dagger of the assassin'. Economic and social ruin became synonymous with Emancipation in the mind of the South.[17]

Labour Control in Belize, Jamaica and the United States of America

Higman argues that emancipation only helped to speed up a process of decline that was already underway by 1834. Abandonment, amalgamation and conversion to livestock-had already begun after the peak year of 1805. The table on the following page supports this argument.

TABLE OF LAND USE IN JAMAICA.

Date of plan	Total area Mean	S.D.	Cane* Mean	S.D.	Guinea grass Mean	S.D.	Common pasture Mean	S.D.	Plantains Mean	S.D.	Woodland Mean	S.D.	Ruinate Mean	S.D.	Provision grounds Mean	S.D.	Number of plan
1750-9	1,946	2,057	381	233	30	42	96	59	—	—	517	681	—	—	29	28	2
1760-9	861	669	272	183	—	—	177	16	19	—	353	577	—	—	50	71	3
1770-9	863	691	277	168	16	22	180	34	37	34	210	441	2	4	85	139	5
1780-9	963	586	190	79	7	13	186	116	19	2	176	305	—	—	353	344	5
1790-9	995	544	263	134	76	79	137	139	5	2	176	157	42	80	290	363	5
1800-9	1,273	816	213	130	121	148	77	19	8	14	118	423	34	57	366	363	22
1810-9	768	369	269	167	78	98	62	63	1	14	319	57	30	52	189	377	14
1820-9	984	630	230	104	78	78	120	112	3	3	14	110	81	112	138	320	14
1830-9	884	425	202	97	111	189	165	143	—	—	106	205	50	112	130	162	25
1840-9	1,217	683	302	145	193	189	194	162	2	—	273	386	293	356	88	143	15
1850-9	1,147	479	312	131	48	122	186	139	—	—	250	318	121	130	161	211	11
1860-9	510	—	174	—	104	—	55	—	—	—	61	—	—	—	,212	—	11
1870-9	1,781	940	331	86	36	41	435	390	—	—	145	566	341	114	,212	433	4
Total	1,036	624	353	131	90	124	157	142	3	10	185	311	81	177	185	260	132

Table 2 Standard Deviation.

*Sugar cane figures show that from 1810 at 269acres to 1829 with 240acres and 202acres in use between 1830 and 1839 that a decline in production had been underway for some time. Other fluctuations up or down merely indicate market forces. No trend exists to show that Emancipation drastically affected sugar production.

Labour Control in Belize, Jamaica and the United States of America

The British Government's difficulties in feeding its own population during the 1840s had as much to do with Jamaican decline as did emancipation. The sugar duties of 1846 removed preferential treatment from Jamaican imports. British traders were now free to buy cheaper sugar from Cuba and Louisiana, where slave systems still flourished, and where larger estates on open plains made cultivation cheaper.[19]. Jamaican sugar was produced in narrow valleys with narrow outlets to the sea, and could not serious compete. By 1864 therefore, more than 15,000 tons of Cuban sugar was being imported into Britain. The 19th century was characterised by stagnation and decline for the Jamaican sugar industry. [20]

fig.4. A sugar estate of the period. Source:National Library of Jamaica.

Clearly in the case of Jamaica, sugar was the chief determinant for labour, but unlike Belizean timber, Jamaican sugar had no monopoly, nor could it compete successfully. Many of Jamaica's problems between 1830 and 1866 stem from this weakness, such as the planter's inability or unwillingness to pay reasonable wages causing labour problems, as did their subsequent use of migrant labour. A continuance of planter control over the legislature, along with a serious drought and hurricane, combined to end the period as it had begun, with a rebellion, this time at Morant Bay in 1865. An event not lost on the planters of the South. The insurrection spread over 75 miles and troops were force-marched, on Governor Eyre's orders, through the mountains from Spanish Town. The result was, 400 men and women were shot or put to death after trial. A further 600 were publicly flogged, 1,000 houses were burned to the ground and the Baptist leader Paul Bogle hanged. [21]

In both Belize and Jamaica, the masters sought to ensure strict control over their former slaves; in the former because of high profits, in the latter because of serious financial difficulties. No one could conceive of an alternative to the plantation system. Any help given by the British was designed to 'shore-up' the system not improve the lot of the Black majority.[22] The introduction of Crown Colony government in 1866 for Jamaica, and 1871 for Belize, was not realized for the benefit of local Blacks, rather because the local oligarchies

fig.5. .Holland Estate near Morant Point. Mid–19th Century.

Source:National Library of Jamaica

feared that radical elements might take over an elected assembly. Whereas the oligarchies might sustain themselves better in councils nominated by Governors. [23] Democratic self-government did not return to Jamaica until 1957 and Belize until 1964.

Labour Control in Belize, Jamaica and the United States of America

The South 1863-1877:

The economic impact of Emancipation on the North was less important as slavery had always been a marginal issue and Negroes a small proportion of the population; so fiscal adjustments were relatively easier. However, in the South the whole situation was confused by war and the initial domination by an outside political force. [24]

The South during Reconstruction

Negroes were determined to exercise their freedom and, as in Jamaica, refused any work organisation that resembled slavery such as the use of 'drivers' or gang-labour. However, overnight emancipation became a dubious boon to many thousands of Blacks who died of hunger and exposure. [25] Many, such as house slaves, were less well off than before and for Blacks and poor whites, the tendency was to sink into debt peonage. A Georgia freedman tells how he was deceived into peonage,

> The storekeeper took us one by one and read to us statements of our accounts [....] I owed $105 [....] But no one would have dared to

> dispute a white man's word [....] There he told us that after we signed acknowledgements of our debts we might go and look for new places. That same night we were rounded up by a constable and ten or twelve white men. The next morning it was explained to us by the two guards [....] that we had made acknowledgement of our indebtedness that we had also agreed to work for the Senator until the debts were paid by hard labour. Really, we had made ourselves lifetime slaves, or peons [....] the truth is we lived in a hell on earth what time we spent in the Senator's peon camp. [26]

Negroes were to find themselves trapped in a system of de facto slavery through this method of indebtedness.

According to Brogan, just as slavery had been primarily an economic institution, emancipation was not something that could be settled by Northern politics but by the 'interplay of impersonal economic forces,' the wishes of Black and white. Unfortunately as the testimony of one Southern white woman shows the results were to be in dialectical response:

> Still the fight was on, the long, long battle that will never end now until one race or the other is absolute. Little by little a resistance sprung up between the newborn freedom-bred Negroes and the former slave owners of the South, a resistance ever punished and ever renewed. [28]

Eventually the plantations became unprofitable, being broken down into either-tenancies or sharecropping. A planter at Abbeville, South Carolina claimed, 'hands could not be hired for wages, I had to yield (to tenancies) or lose my labour'. His plantation was divided into plots of 25 acres at a rent of four bales of cotton per year. One of the former slaves demands had been a limited working day and no more dawn to dusk production. Nine to ten hour days became the rule but this had the consequence of reducing the labour supply by a third, and thus crop production by a third, when the price was dropping and cotton was suffering competition from India and Egypt. [29]

However, the economic system that developed was one dominated by debt. The planter class was, according to Brogan, 'disgraced, bankrupt, disfranchised and unpopular', but still in control of the land. To regain some capital they had been forced to take out mortgages.[30] Likewise the Negro and poor white relied upon loans from local merchants in order to purchase supplies, particularly fertilizer, because the land was becoming single-crop dominated. Subsistence farming had been moved over to make way for more cotton, which further depleted the soil, requiring expensive fertilizers such as guano to generate fresh crops. [31] Although other crops were grown in the South such as sugar in Louisiana, single-crop domination had become as prevalent here as in Belize or Jamaica and the chief determinant of labour; subject to all the vagaries of the weather, market forces, and competition that shifted the mood, of Belize Town dwellers. [32]

In all three areas, the workers became, to greater and lesser degrees, dispossessed and dependent on those who held the monopoly in land control. The major difference being that Belize and Jamaica were colonies populated mainly by Negroes. They could be neglected or developed at will with no serious trouble to the metropolis. Geographically, however the South was an integral part of the United States as were its majority population of whites and its minorities. Though often exploited by Northern business, the South benefited from a belated industrialisation process, although few of the benefits found their way to the Negro, or poor white.

Peter Hitchen

References

1. O. Nigel Bolland, 'Labour Control in Post-Abolition Belize,' *Journal of Belizean Affairs* (1979) 9, 21.

2. O. Nigel Bolland, 'Labour Control in Post-Abolition Belize' (1979) 22.

3. O. Nigel Bolland, 'Systems of Domination after Slavery,' *Comparative Studies in Society and History* (1981) 23, 4, 593.

4. William A. Green's 'The Perils of Comparative History', *Comparative Studies in Society and History* (1984) 26, 1, 112.

5. O. Nigel Bolland, 'Labour Control in Post-Abolition Belize' (1979) 22.

6. William A. Green's 'The Perils of Comparative History' (1984) 112.

7. O. Nigel Bolland, 'Labour Control in Post-Abolition Belize' (1979) 24.

8. A. R. Gibbs, *British Honduras: An Historical and Descriptive Account of the Colony from its Settlement*, 1670. (London 1883). 114.

9. O. Nigel Bolland, 'Labour Control in Post-Abolition Belize' (1979) 22.

10. B. W. Higman, 'The Spatial Economy of Jamaican Sugar Plantations', *Journal of Historical Geography* (1987) 13, 1,18.

11. Ibid, 17.

12. William A. Green's 'The Perils of Comparative History' (1984) 113.

13. William A. Green's 'The Perils of Comparative History' (1984) 121.

14. F. R. Augier et al (eds) *The Making of the West Indies* (Trinidad 1950) 185.

15. G. Beckford, M. Witter, *Small Garden Bitter Weed: The Political Economy of Change and Struggle in Jamaica* (Jamaica 1982) 37.

16. B. W. Higman, 'The Spatial Economy of Jamaican Sugar Plantations' (1987) 17-24.

17. Joe Wilkins, 'Window on Freedom: South Carolina's Response to British West Indian Slave Emancipation', *South Carolina Historical Magazine* (1984) 85, 2, 143.

18. B. W. Higman, 'The Spatial Economy of Jamaican Sugar Plantations' (1987) 19.

19. F. R. Augier et al (eds) *The Making of the West Indies* (Trinidad 1950) iv, 193, 212.

20. B. W. Higman, 'The Spatial Economy of Jamaican Sugar Plantations' (1987) 10.

[21] Michael Craton, 'Continuity not Change: The incidence of unrest among ex-Slaves in the British West Indies, 1838-1876', *Slavery and Abolition* (1988) 9, 2, 153-154.

[22] Ibid, 163.

[23] Ibid, 154.

[24] Stanley L. Engerman, 'Economic adjustments to Emancipation in the United States and the British West Indies', *Journal Of Interdisciplinary History* (1982) 13, 2, 192.

[25] T. A. Bailey, *Probing America's Past Vol 2* (Massachusetts 1973) 416.

[26] 'The life story of a Negro peon', in Hamilton Holt, *The Life Stories of Undistinguished Americans: as told by themselves* (London 1990) 119.

[27] Hugh Brogan, *The Penguin History of the United States* (London 1985) 368.

[28] The Life Story of a Southern White Woman', in Hamilton Holt, *The Life Stories of Undistinguished Americans: as told by themselves* (London 1990) 212.

'The life story of a Negro peon', in Hamilton Holt, *The Life Stories of Undistinguished Americans: as told by themselves* (London 1990) 114.

[29] Lacey K. Ford, 'Rednecks and Merchants: Economic Development and Social Tensions in the South Carolina Up-Country, 1865-1900', *Journal of American History* (1984) 72, 2, 304.

[30] Hugh Brogan, *The Penguin History of the United States*, 368.

[31] Lacey K. Ford, 'Rednecks and Merchants', *Journal of American History* (1984) 304.

[32] William A. Green's 'The Perils of Comparative History' (1984) 112.

Peter Hitchen

2
Land Monopoly

This chapter shall illustrate and analyse the fundamental area of control which was the first consideration of the masters in denying ex-slaves their freedom, and the first consideration for the ex-slaves in establishing that freedom; revealing how the availability of land was critical to the success or failure of its systems of Labour control; which rapidly emerged from the outset of emancipation. On this matter historians agree; William A. Green and Stanley Engerman support the relationship between land and population density as being the vital factor in the transition from slavery to wage labour. However, Bolland whilst accepting the importance of population density, adds that the actual control of land is crucial, supplying an additional element for a more complete analysis. Therefore the latter's theses will be largely applied to the subject of labour controls. Finally an attempt will be made to understand the motives of both the British and United States governments as separate from the local ruling classes. [1]

Generally, the literature on Jamaica and Belize covering the 19th century has divided into two periods: slavery before abolition and freedom after emancipation. However, this perpetuates the illusion that labour power was suddenly freed as a commodity. Bolland suggests that some, 'uncritically conceptualise post-emancipation colonies as free'. [2] Pete Daniel asserts in support of this argument that nowhere have masters ever submitted passively to freedom, and in the case of the Caribbean and the South the planters never willingly surrendered control.[3] Green adds, 'Freedom was grafted upon an exclusive system which was ill-equipped in sentiment and character to administer a free society'. [4] Clearly then, there was a period of transition that distinguishes between Emancipation as an event and emancipation as a human social condition. [5]

In connection with this, there was continuity between slavery and freedom where masters sought out new methods of coercion, as the ex-slaves demanded new forms of freedom. Bolland adds, 'Domination persists even while the relations of domination change [....]The ability of a minority of whites to monopolize land is the common denominator'.[6] Land control was, therefore, of paramount importance to both masters and former slaves, with both groups expressing their concern over who should possess Crown or spare lands. Although the Belizean ex-slaves had for long been used as foresters in the mahogany trade, involving scattered work gangs, they too had been used in limited agricultural work on their own provision grounds, likewise the plantation based Jamaican worker. Nevertheless, the masters were determined to keep the land from the slaves (to inhibit the development of an independent peasantry). [7]

Labour Control in Belize, Jamaica and the United States of America

Herein, the local authorities were supported by the Colonial Office. Lord Normanby wrote to MacDonald, Superintendent of Belize, on 22 April 1839 ordering him to cease the 'gratuitous granting of land', as this would discourage 'labour for wages'. [8] The former slaves could ill-afford to buy the land and none at all was sold to them up to 1855. By 1868, the total was said to be 'utterly insignificant'. [9] Much of the land eventually passed by purchase to the settlers. Similarly, a Colonial Office memo of 7 January had expressed the fear that parts of the West Indies could suffer difficulties as had been seen among white labourers,

> in the Western United States; in the British North American Provinces; in the Colony of the Cape of Good Hope and in the Australian Settlement [where] the facility of procuring land has invariably created a proportionate difficulty in obtaining hired labourers. [10]

Evidently, the British Government was well aware of the potential economic crisis that might occur. The immediate fear of the mahogany lords (well justified in the light of later events) was that they might not be able to sustain the boom in timber exports should the Negroes desert the logging camps particularly as Belizean timber production suffered from an inherent labour shortage.[11] Jamaica, however, was already under intense competition from the East India lobby in Parliament over the ending of special trade regulations for the West Indies, and a return to free-trade. Cuba also threatened severe competition due to her retention of slavery.[12] Thus the problem was critical, for Jamaica, unlike Belize, did not simply fear losing a lucrative market but seriously considered the possibility of total economic collapse.[13]

It was to the advantage of the Belize settlers that their country was not yet a Crown Colony. This meant limited powers for the Superintendent [than if he had been a Governor] having little effective authority over the magistrates; who also happened to be the major landowners. Consequently, the men who controlled the mahogany trade were able to buy out most of the spare arable land from the Crown, even though in 1838 it had originally been designated for gratuitous distribution to former slaves. Much remained idle during the mid-Victorian period.[14] Belizean ex-slaves, therefore, were compelled by a lack of alternative employment to remain with foresting, minimising though not eradicating resistance in Belize for a great deal of the 19th century.

Unlike Jamaica, whose former slaves were always aware of the availability of agricultural land, and where protest began from the earliest months after abolition. The Governor of Jamaica, the Marquis of Sligo in a letter to King William IV, spoke highly of the successful transition from slave labour, but the Governor then goes on to report a passive resistance in the St.Ann's district

> They have committed no overt act whatever but doggedly refuse to work, submitting, with an appearance of pleasure, to their punishment, their comrades exhorting them to bear it for the sake of freedom. They all have said, 'King William had given them free and they would take it.' Fearing that this might spread if not put an end to at once, the moment I received notification of this state of affairs, I sent off Colonel Macleod to Ocho Rios.[15]

Sligo entered into more detail three days later to Thomas Spring-Rice, Secretary to the Colonies,

> I received a letter by express from Mr. Walker the member for St Anne to say that the apprentices on his estate and those around him had refused to work without payment. Had threatened him with their own law and shown the most insubordinate spirit, unless a stop was made it might spread it might spread all over the island and create considerable embarrassment.

Remarking on the presence of Colonel MacLeod,

> But strange to say even with that effect it became necessary to punish a vast number of the Negroes as well as by flogging, as confinement to the workhouse; when asked to work they uniformly refused [saying] that they were to be free, and that we were concealing the law.[16]

This last point is in reference to the apprenticeship system which was seen as virtual slavery and which is borne out by the acts of flogging and incarceration that must have seemed indistinguishable from the days of slavery. What does differ from slavery is the potential for widespread strike action, hardly imaginable during bondage, emphasising a new found 'freedom' of expression not possible without access to other forms of livelihood, in this case arable land which was not available to all but gave them a sense of freedom that might be attained.

By 1842 Lord Elgin was writing to Lord Stanley at the Colonial Office complaining that,

> The want of continuous labour is still very much felt on the estates as the labourers work very irregularly, without any regard to the wants or wishes of their employers. [17]

Whilst illustrating the lack of labour Lord Elgin's tone unwittingly reveals something of the British Government's attitude towards the Negroes. Elgin could not understand why former slaves should not have any regard for ex-slaveholders.

The Baptist missionary Reverend William Knibb played an important role in procuring land for former slaves. By November of 1838 he had bought 1,000 acres in the mountains for parcelling out to Negroes. By 1845, Knibb stated that 19,000 ex-slaves had purchased land and were building their own homes.[18] Knox cites the attitudes of planters,

> While freedmen supposedly 'vegetated' on their subsistence plots the sugar plantations would cease to be productive for want of an adequate labour force to cultivate and harvest the canes, [19]

In addition, Jamaican masters were struggling to maintain profits amid fierce competition while much of their own land was mortgaged. They were not in any financial state to begin a wholesale purchasing of land , whereas among the ex-slaves many could at least find the resources for a small subsistence plot. [20] Unlike Belize, as Bolland explained, 'consists of about 8,600 square miles of land. In the 1830s, the population did not rise above 4,000 persons'. [21] So the population density of Belize was very low, one person for every two square miles approximately. This should mean similar difficulties in line with Jamaica, but due to the effective control of land by the masters, they were able to maintain domination over the workforce.

Violence was the essential difference between the transition to emancipation in the South, through the Civil War, and the relatively peaceful transition in the British West Indies. There were other differences, such as the £20,000,000 compensation provided for the confiscation of the British planter's property; his slaves. Also, the Southern white elites had the advantage of being part of a majority group. Jamaican landlords were mostly absentees lacking the cultural stake in their community that existed in the South. Nevertheless, in each there was a strong desire to maintain a white hegemony. In the South, this erupted in extra-legal violence after the breakdown of paternalism, an issue that will be discussed in Chapter 4.

In view of the differences, it is interesting to note that many attempts to subjugate the Negroes initially followed a similar path to that of the Caribbean. Primary among these was the battle for the control of land. As Maldwyn Jones claims, 'What they [the Negroes] wanted most was land, education, and the vote, in that order'. [22] Many Negroes believed that land would be given to them. The report extract below of General Rufus Saxton is one of many cited in Fleming's 'Documents',

> The impression is universal among the freedmen that they are to have the abandoned and confiscated lands, in homesteads of forty acres in January next. It is understood that previous to the termination of the late war the Negroes heard from those in rebellion that it was the purpose of our government to divide up the Southern plantations among them---6 December 1865. [23]

Land was widely recognised as being essential to the Negroes' future prosperity. The *New York Independent* newspaper gave its solid support

Labour Control in Belize, Jamaica and the United States of America

> The Negro question solves itself. [...] the easiest of all difficult problems. Land and the ballot-land that he may support his family the ballot that he may support the state. Grant these to the Negro and he will trouble the nation no more'. [24]

But the most prophetic words came from Secretary of War Stanton in which he concluded, 'without land reform a system of serfdom would develop'. [25]

The concept of ownership had not escaped the 20 Negro leaders who met Stanton and General Sherman in Savannah. The latter were asked how the Negro people could best stand on their own feet, replying, 'The way we can best take care of ourselves is to have land and till it by our own labour'. [26] It has been necessary here to show that there had been a diverse body of opinion on the subject, drawing similar conclusions.

In view of the well-publicised views of the pro-Negroes it would not be surprising to learn that the opponents of emancipation were equally aware of the land factor. During the debate on the Land Reform Bill, a leading Democrat made the following speech,

> A division of rich man's lands among the landless would give a shock to our whole social and political system from which it would hardly recover without the loss of liberty. (A proposal) in which provision is made for the violation of a greater number of the principles of good government and for the opening of a deeper sink of corruption has never been submitted to a legislature. [27]

Clearly to Congress the 'loss of liberty' during slavery was not a sufficient 'sink of corruption' and the Land Reform Bill was defeated; largely due to the expectations of business interests among Republicans, who saw property less Negroes as the perfect reserve army of labour for Northern industries and investment in Southern cotton. Stamp claims that the failure of land reform was probably responsible for the ultimate failure of Reconstruction. [28]

Previous attempts to assign land, through the Freedman's Bureau had failed. The 'Christian General', Oliver Otis Howard, headed the Bureau. They were authorised to grant 'not more than forty acres', of lands that had been abandoned. This meant enough for 20,000 families. Advertisements for these grants ran throughout the autumn of 1865, however, hardly any grants were made, chiefly due to the intervention of President Johnson. The President believed fervently in his policy of 'home-rule', entrusting Southern States and all their inhabitants to former Southern leaders who requested pardons. Johnson finally restored all the lands of one B. B. Leake and on the back of some relevant correspondence instructed the land commissioners, in his own hand as follows, 'The same action will be had in all similar cases'. William S.McFeely sums up the consequences of Johnson's actions, 'In this simple way, Johnson destroyed the first programme, for providing a firm economic base for Black Americans ever undertaken by the government'. [29] Howard did not attempt to reverse Johnson's decision but strangely accepted an opportunity to tour the South preaching to whites and to incredulous Blacks that the Freedman's Bureau really stood for a stable wage labour system; the antitheses of land ownership.

It is not the purpose here to cite the many attempts to provide land but to illustrate something of the importance placed therein by all sections of the community. Although here, land grants were frustrated at the highest level. At Davis Bend, Mississippi, government officers seized six plantations, one of which had formerly belonged to Jefferson Davis. After two years, the grants had extended to over 1,800 Negroes, who were organised into companies and partnerships, ending that year with profits of $159,000. Successfully dispelling any idea of the shiftless Negro.[30] However Johnson, in his zeal for 'home-rule' used his executive powers to side-step Congress by pardoning the original owners and restoring their land, even though his original amnesty proclamation disallowed certain categories of Southerner from a pardon. For example:

> First: All who are or shall have been pretended civil or diplomatic officers [....] of the pretended Confederate government.

> Second: All who left judicial stations under the United States to aid the rebellion [….]

> Fifth: All Who resigned or tendered resignations of their commissions [….] Thirteenth: All persons who have voluntarily participated in the said rebellion and the estimated value of whose taxable property is over $20,000. [31]

The latter clause would seem to have excluded the likes of Jeff Davis, but

Johnson left what amounted to an escape route:

> PROVIDED, That special application may be made to the President for pardon by any person belonging to the excepted classes and such clemency may be liberally extended as may be consistent with the facts [….] **with restoration**Error! Bookmark not defined. **of all rights of property**. (Emphasis mine). [32]

At this' point it is worth considering that Johnson referred to

Reconstruction as 'Restoration' [33] which has the meaning of returning to old

values rather than rebuilding on new principles. Coupled with the knowledge

that Johnson was a Southerner, who had remained loyal to the Union, he is

revealed as a man who is more concerned with the Restoration of that Union

than with Negro rights. After a meeting with Frederick Douglass and other

Black leaders a reporter heard him say to his secretary, 'Those damned sons of

bitches thought they had me in a trap. I know that damned Douglass; he's just

like any other nigger; and he would sooner cut a white man's throat than not'. [34]

We can see from the overall evidence that the executive authority was no friend

of the Negro. C .Van Woodward wrote,

> There was extra land in the South, but that which was most available was quickly snatched from their grasp by the frustration of the Freedmen's Bureau plans for the distribution of abandoned lands, and the less available land was beyond their reach for lack of capital. [35]

With the Restoration of land to the white hierarchies of the South

political power soon followed and the fate of the Blacks was effectively sealed.

William Green states:

> Submissive and disciplined labour was the pivot upon which the whole apparatus of planter power depended. West Indian oligarchs intended to perpetuate their exclusive control over the political, judicial, and law enforcement machinery of the colonies as a means of regulating the lives and labours of former slaves. [36]

Daniel suggests, accurately, to change a few words and the description would fit the South. [37]

Nevertheless, Jamaican planters were not as successful as Southern planters, or indeed other West Indians, in perpetuating involuntary servitude among freedmen. Due to a lack of financial means most of the spare land was out of the planter's control. Therefore, at the time of Emancipation this was a minor weakness, which eventually grew more serious and instigated the downfall of the planter system. Belize, however, had neither the difficulties of Jamaica nor the aftermath of war and defeat that enflamed the passions of the South. The masters had a secure hold over land, and consequently the Negro workforce, which would only be affected by a depression in the mahogany trade. Throughout, the Negro's main concern had been economic independence through land grants. Conversely, the immediate concern of the masters was to return the Negro to a state of economic dependence as quickly as possible.

Labour Control in Belize, Jamaica and the United States of America

References

1. William A. Green, 'The Perils of Comparative History', *Comparative Studies in Society and History* (1984) 26, 1, 112-119.

Stanley L. Engerman, 'Economic Changes and Contract Labour in the British Caribbean', *Explorations in Economic History* (1984) 21, 2, 133-150.

O. Nigel Bolland, *Colonialism and Resistance in Belize: Essays in Historical Sociology* (Benque Viejo del Carmen Belize 1988).

2. O. Nigel Bolland, 'Systems of Domination after Slavery,' *Comparative Studies in Society and History* (1981) 23, 4, 592.

3. Pete Daniel, 'The Metamorphosis of Slavery, 1865-1900', *Journal of American History* (1979) 66, 1, 93.

4. William Green, *British Slave Emancipation: the Sugar Colonies and the great experiment* (Oxford 1976) 95.

5. Bolland in William A. Green, 'The Perils of Comparative History', *Comparative Studies in Society and History* (1984) 113.

6. O. Nigel Bolland, 'Reply to William A. Green's 'The Perils of Comparative History', *Comparative Studies in Society and History* (1984) 26, 1, 120-125.

O. Nigel Bolland, 'Labour Control in Post-Abolition Belize' *Journal of Belizean Affairs* (1979) 9, 22.

7. Ibid, 22.

8. Lord Normanby to Superintendent MacDonald, 22 April 1839, Belize Archives 15.

9. Ibid.

10. Heads of a Plan for the Abolition of Negro Slavery. CO 320/817.

11. O. Nigel Bolland, 'Labour Control in Post-Abolition Belize' (1979) 9, 23.

12. William Green, *British Slave Emancipation: the Sugar Colonies and the great experiment* (Oxford 1976) 38.

13. Stanley L. Engerman, 'Economic Changes and Contract Labour in the British Caribbean' (1984) 137.

14. O. Nigel Bolland, 'Labour Control in Post-Abolition Belize' (1979) 21-35.

15. Sligo to King William IV. 10 August 1834. 'The Sligo Papers', Manuscript Collection of the National Library of Jamaica.

16. Sligo to Thomas Spring-Rice. 13 August 1834. 'The Sligo Papers', Manuscript Collection of the National Library of Jamaica.

17. Lord Elgin to Lord Stanley. CO 137/263, No.6.

18. Jean Besson, 'Land Tenures in the Free Villages of Trelawney, Jamaica', *Slavery and Abolition* (1984) 15, 1, 7.

19. A. J. G. Knox, 'Opportunities and Opposition: The Rise of Jamaica's Black Peasantry and the Nature of Planter Resistance', *Canadian Review of Sociology and Anthropology* (1977) 14, 4, 384.

20. Ibid.

21.William Green, *British Slave Emancipation: the Sugar Colonies and the great experiment* (Oxford 1976) 600.

22. Maldwyn Jones, *The Limits of Liberty: American History 1607 - 1980* (Oxford. 1983) 254.

23. Senate Executive Document. No.27. 39 Congress, 1 Session, page 140. Report of General Rufus Saxton, assistant commissioner for South Carolina. December 6, 1865) in Walter Fleming (eds) *Documentary History of Reconstruction* (Massachusetts. 1960). Document No. 354.

24. *New York Independent Newspaper* 1867 in Kenneth M. Stampp, *The Era of Reconstruction: America after the Civil War* (London. 1965) 128.

25. Speech by Secretary of War Stanton in Kenneth M. Stampp, *The Era of Reconstruction*, 125.

26. Ibid, 123.

27. Congressional speech on the Land Reform Bill in Kenneth M. Stampp, *The Era of Reconstruction*, 130.

28. Ibid, 129-130.

29. William S. McFeely, 'Unfinished Business: The Freedmen's Bureau and Federal Action in Race Relations', in N. Huggins et al, *Key Issues in the Afro-American Experience*, Vol. 2 (San Diego 1971) 12.

30. *New York Independent Newspaper* 1867 in Kenneth M. Stampp, *The Era of Reconstruction*, 125.

31. Richardson, Messages and Papers,Vol vi, page 310. May 29 1865. in Walter Fleming (eds) *Documentary History of Reconstruction* (Massachusetts 1960). Document No.170.

32. Ibid.

33. Hugh Brogan, *The Penguin History of the United States* (London 1985) 361.

34. Albert Castel, *The Presidency of Andrew Johnson* (Lawrence 1979) 64.

35. C. Vann Woodward in Pete Daniel, 'The Metamorphosis of Slavery, 1865-1900' (1979) 93 – 94.

36. Green in Pete Daniel, 'The Metamorphosis of Slavery, 1865-1900' (1979) 94.

37. Pete Daniel, 'The Metamorphosis of Slavery, 1865-1900' (1979) 94.

Peter Hitchen

Peter Hitchen

3
SYSTEMS OF LABOUR CONTROL

I n order to undermine any power the Negro labourer may have possessed, the planters and mahogany chiefs sought to establish the use of a contract system, supported by the pernicious use of advances. Additionally, in each area immigrant workers were used with varying degrees of success.

For the mahogany foresters of Belize the labour supply, rather than its control, had always been a problem. This was largely due to Belize' remoteness from the slave markets, and the high premium given to male physical strength in foresting. The value of Belizean ex-slaves is revealed in the compensation rates provided by the British Government. £53 6s 9d was a higher rate than in all the sugar islands. Jamaican slaves had been valued at £19 5s 4d each. [1]

Similarly, Jamaica and the South suffered difficulties, though not from initial shortages, rather from a desertion of the estates. In particular, many women had refused to return to fieldwork. Bolland, in discussing African continuities in the Caribbean claims that familial stability with the woman at home was maintained throughout slavery in Belize. Although this was disrupted in Jamaica it is not difficult to accept that such African continuities were maintained in the thoughts of Jamaican women; especially as many Jamaican ex-slaves were only one or two generations removed from their African lands. [2] Augier states that many Jamaican women never returned to outside employment. Seeing manual labour as 'the mark of servitude' they usually worked their own land, cared for the home, and raised a family. [3]

Following the Civil War an attempt was made in the South to work the freedmen on a free wage-labour basis. But the Negroes could not always be relied upon to be present at the all-important harvest time, whereas the planter required a guaranteed labour force. [4] One planter commented 'nine freedmen will not do the work of six slaves'. [5]

Post-1838 in Jamaica saw similar problems, but here they were characterised by the bitterness and retrenchment of the planter oligarchy. Swithin Wilmot reveals a contrast of approaches between master and labourer, 'Masters got together to work out a system of control whereas ex-slaves wished to discuss means of getting down to work'.[6] Jamaican workers were quite prepared to strike for equitable terms. As the planter was no longer required to feed and clothe the entire Negro family then the Negro worker decided that one-shilling and six pence was a fare daily rate for himself, simply to maintain his former standard of living under slavery. The planters at Bushy Park offered seven pence a day, and demanded two days work as rent for cottages and provision grounds. This was on August 8 1838, only one week after final Emancipation. It took the intervention of the Governor, Sir Lionel Smith to break the deadlock. His plan of one shilling a day and free rent became acceptable to both sides.

Labour Control in Belize, Jamaica and the United States of America

Similar events took place in Trelawney and St. James but Smith's plan soon became the standard contract with special terms for various skilled workers.[7] Wherever Negroes were treated in any serious measure as in their former condition they deserted the estates. During October of 1838 on Green Park estate, of a workforce of 404, only 35 were at work. Perhaps even former slaves were willing participants in a shift to a capitalist mode of production. Now that freedom had been achieved, a corollary of that freedom was the right to refuse to work. [8] It would appear that former slaves and the distant commercial interests in London had a more complete understanding of new economic system than the local plantation attorneys. Apart from the derisory daily rates, which were eventually increased with other plantations, the Green Park attorney had attempted to retain 'drivers' in the fields as supervisors. Other plantations such as Tilson and Morant, and the Plantain Garden River District suffered similar difficulties. [9] The desire on the part of the Negroes to act with autonomy, combined with their freedom of movement, was clearly a major weakness for the planters.

The loss of labour to subsistence plots or because of unsatisfactory conditions left the Jamaican planters in a more difficult position than their counterparts in Belize and the South. Workers simply moved to another plantation at the end of a contract period. Even then the labourer refused to sign new terms without the presence of the Colonial Office appointed Stipendiary Magistrates. Whenever the planters arbitrarily altered the terms of a contract, the workers struck. One planter Charles Darling, held the rare, but wise view of 'civil treatment with cash wages regularly paid'.[10]

However, in Belize the Colonial Office was bringing pressure to bear to regulate the duties of master and servant. Contracts had already existed in Belize for the free-Negro workers. The following extract from the Clerk of the Court's report supports this whilst revealing the system's inherent unfairness,

Peter Hitchen

> It is the practice to enter into contract by which they hire themselves generally for six to twelve months [....]. It is in the enforcement of these contracts however, that the great evil lies. There is no law on the subject further than what custom has sanctioned. That custom has been, where the servant has failed in his Contract the Master [can] have him summarily punished by imprisonment and Public whipping. If the breach of Contract lay with the master [over payments] the Servant could only sue the Master as in a common debt. [11]

This treatment amounted to a complete denial of justice, as no labourer could afford to spend months in Belize Town prohibited from leaving, or from making another contract, with all the subsequent loss of earnings involved.

Thus, fair sounding regulations were drawn up which resembled the old system, but empowering magistrates to fine employers for withholding payments and insisting that all contracts should be in writing. Nevertheless, evidence shows that the application of the law was slanted towards controlling the workforce. An amnesty on 1 August 1838 freed all prisoners. Four months later 34 of 103 had been found guilty of 'breach of contract'. One of these was Pedro Chabia, who received six-months hard labour on Public Works. By 1848, the law was amended to allow for the forcible removal of an employee, without warrant, by his employer or agent, to his place of work. [12] This was an effective mechanism of labour control inherited from slavery and continued, in Belize, until well into the 20th century.

By 1867 in the South forms of contract had arisen as either the sharecropping or the tenancy system. York County planter Iredell Jones reveals some limits to the absolute power of the Southern planter class. He confessed that, 'the cropping system has been found by experience to be most unwieldy and unsatisfactory'.[13] These limits on power are similar to the Jamaican planter's predicament; partly due to their difficult financial states and partly the imposition of a higher and distant authority, namely the Federal and Colonial government's directives regarding the treatment of Negroes. The Negro freedmen entered into annual contracts to participate in collective farming for a share of the crop, with a portion paid monthly, and the remainder kept until after the harvest to coerce them not to break the contract. Ralph Shlomowitz claims that the problem here for planters and workers was the 'free-rider'; shirkers who necessitated others doing their share. Offenders were fined, a practise still existing in 1877 when an article in the *New York Times* stated, 'This charging takes the place of whipping in slavery';[14] A remark that succinctly acknowledges the shift in systems of control.

Increasingly Negroes demanded more influence over their own work time, as much as the landlords wished to overcome the problem of monitoring workers. This was achieved as cropping was scaled down to family groups. The positive stimulus of family production rendered monitoring redundant and fining minimal. [15] Clear distinctions in law, in line with de facto differences already existing, had been made between sharecroppers and tenant farmers. The former was a wage labourer and employee with no legal interest in the crop. The latter however, had legal title and could go anywhere for his supplies. However, the reality favoured the planter who, in the case of Negroes and not poor whites, refused to allow a tenancy that did not purchase supplies from the landlord. Nevertheless, tenancies were the favoured mode of operation for both planters and Negroes; the latter because tenancy was the furthest removed from the old slavery methods. Negroes were the preferred type of labour as this testimony from an Alabama Planter reveals,

> White labour is totally unsuited to our methods, our manners, and our accommodations [....] No other labourer [than the Negro] of whom I have any knowledge, would be as cheerful, or so contented on four pounds of meat and a pack of meal a week in a little log cabin 14'x16' with cracks in it large enough to afford a free passage to a large size cat.[16]

Although Black tolerance of his conditions might be influenced by the legally enforce terms of their contracts. As a Negro from Georgia testifies,

Peter Hitchen

We learned that we could not break our contract for any reason and. go and hire ourselves to someone else [....] We could be run down by bloodhounds arrested without process of law and be returned to our employer, who, according to the contract, might beat us brutally or administer any other kind of punishment that he thought proper. In other words, we had sold ourselves into slavery. [17]

This remark from a Mississippi planter simply but clearly reveals why Negro labour was preferred, 'We can boss him and that is what we Southern folk like'.[18] General Swayne says the planters felt the need for support for the contract system from the Freedmen's Bureau,

> I found the contract system established here--The planters liked it, and so vigorously demanded contracts that there was danger they would not undertake to plant at all without them. Idleness was extremely prevalent, and contracts might answer to restrain their disposition.[19]

Thus the law was developed similarly to that in force in Belize, and Jamaica where there was an insistence upon, a written contract with two white persons witnessing, protection for the recovery of wages, enforcement of a twelve month minimum period, and arrest, imprisonment and hard labour for breaking an agreement, linked and supported by harsh vagrancy laws. While punishments for Southern Blacks were usually physical, poor whites were generally fined; for it was considered politically dangerous to administer physical punishment on whites. [20] But redress in the courts was worse for the Southern Negro than elsewhere. They could not testify against whites, while a jury would be made up of all whites. These laws were temporarily abandoned under Radical Reconstruction, but were reintroduced under the 'Redeemers' from 1877 onwards. An extract from the laws relating to labour contracts is reproduced from Fleming's Documents at figure 6 below. [21] As Shofner suggests, this series of racist and repressive laws known generally as the 'Black-Codes' all made economic sense to the 'firebrands of the old Confederacy'. [22] The withdrawal of these laws was to create a long period of violence inflicted upon Blacks.

Peter Hitchen

In Jamaica, the laws of tenancy were exploited by the landlords as a means of control. Under the Smith agreement, the workers had settled for a lower daily rate of pay in exchange free rent, but under the law, this equalled no tenancy. Thus planters regularly used the rent issue, to coerce labour; threatening to evict at any time even though the worker was in possession of a

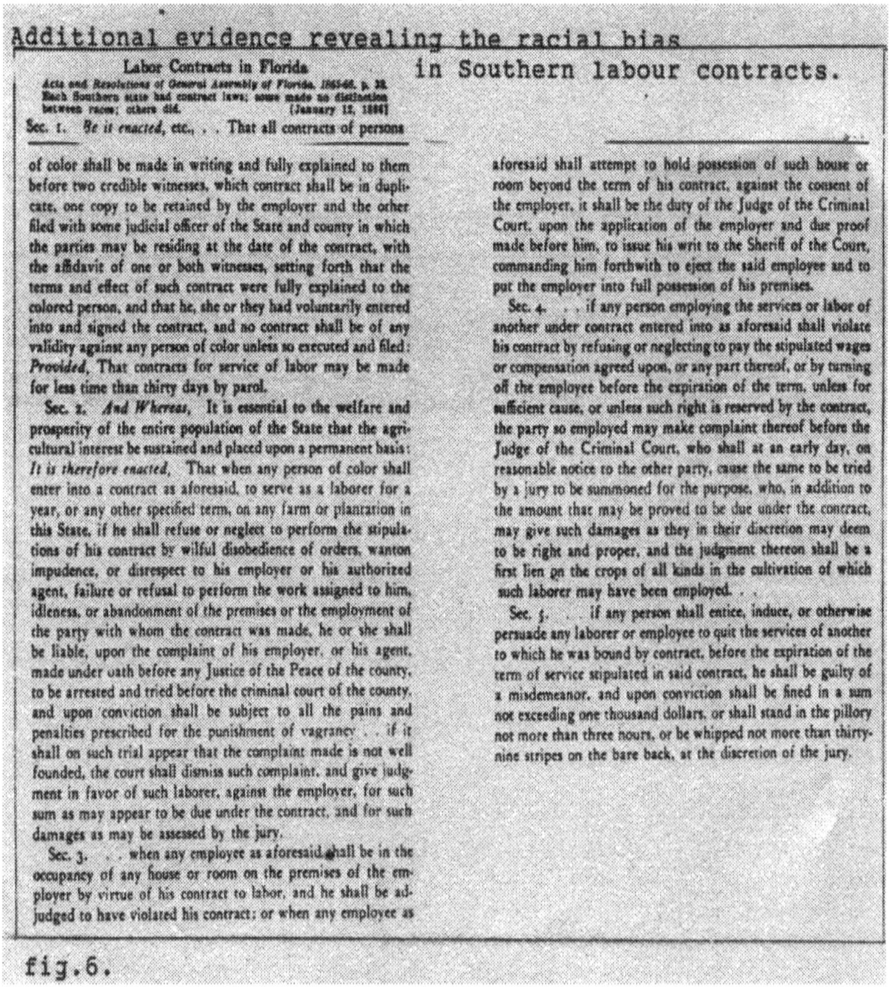

Additional evidence revealing the racial bias in Southern labour contracts.

Labor Contracts in Florida

Acts and Resolutions of General Assembly of Florida, 1865-66, p. 32. Such Southern state had contract laws; some made no distinction between races; others did. [January 12, 1866]

Sec. 1. *Be it enacted,* etc., . . . That all contracts of persons of color shall be made in writing and fully explained to them before two credible witnesses, which contract shall be in duplicate, one copy to be retained by the employer and the other filed with some judicial officer of the State and county in which the parties may be residing at the date of the contract, with the affidavit of one or both witnesses, setting forth that the terms and effect of such contract were fully explained to the colored person, and that he, she or they had voluntarily entered into and signed the contract, and no contract shall be of any validity against any person of color unless so executed and filed: *Provided,* That contracts for service of labor may be made for less time than thirty days by parol.

Sec. 2. *And Whereas,* It is essential to the welfare and prosperity of the entire population of the State that the agricultural interest be sustained and placed upon a permanent basis: *It is therefore enacted,* That when any person of color shall enter into a contract as aforesaid, to serve as a laborer for a year, or any other specified term, on any farm or plantation in this State, if he shall refuse or neglect to perform the stipulations of his contract by wilful disobedience of orders, wanton impudence, or disrespect to his employer or his authorized agent, failure or refusal to perform the work assigned to him, idleness, or abandonment of the premises or the employment of the party with whom the contract was made, he or she shall be liable, upon the complaint of his employer, or his agent, made under oath before any Justice of the Peace of the county, to be arrested and tried before the criminal court of the county, and upon conviction shall be subject to all the pains and penalties prescribed for the punishment of vagrancy . . if it shall on such trial appear that the complaint made is not well founded, the court shall dismiss such complaint, and give judgment in favor of such laborer, against the employer, for such sum as may appear to be due under the contract, and for such damages as may be assessed by the jury.

Sec. 3. . . when any employee as aforesaid shall be in the occupancy of any house or room on the premises of the employer by virtue of his contract to labor, and he shall be adjudged to have violated his contract; or when any employee as aforesaid shall attempt to hold possession of such house or room beyond the term of his contract, against the consent of the employer, it shall be the duty of the Judge of the Criminal Court, upon the application of the employer and due proof made before him, to issue his writ to the Sheriff of the Court, commanding him forthwith to eject the said employee and to put the employer into full possession of his premises.

Sec. 4. . . if any person employing the services or labor of another under contract entered into as aforesaid shall violate his contract by refusing or neglecting to pay the stipulated wages or compensation agreed upon, or any part thereof, or by turning off the employee before the expiration of the term, unless for sufficient cause, or unless such right is reserved by the contract, the party so employed may make complaint thereof before the Judge of the Criminal Court, who shall at an early day, on reasonable notice to the other party, cause the same to be tried by a jury to be summoned for the purpose, who, in addition to the amount that may be proved to be due under the contract, may give such damages as they in their discretion may deem to be right and proper, and the judgment thereon shall be a first lien on the crops of all kinds in the cultivation of which such laborer may have been employed. .

Sec. 5. . . if any person shall entice, induce, or otherwise persuade any laborer or employee to quit the services of another to which he was bound by contract, before the expiration of the term of service stipulated in said contract, he shall be guilty of a misdemeanor, and upon conviction shall be fined in a sum not exceeding one thousand dollars, or shall stand in the pillory not more than three hours, or be whipped not more than thirty-nine stripes on the bare back, at the discretion of the jury.

fig.6.

legal contract of employment. [23] This would then render them liable to arrest for vagrancy and sentenced to toil on public works or provide their masters with free labour. [24]

Labour Control in Belize, Jamaica and the United States of America

Further protections for the supply of labour in the South were developed during the mid-1860s, alongside cropping and tenancy. A system of advances which created indebtedness and ultimately peonage. A Negro peon provides a valuable testimony into how he was deceived into debt servitude,

> At the end of the fifth year the Senator suggested that I sign up a contract for ten years, then, he said, we wouldn't have to fix up papers every year. [The Senator] had established a large store, [....] all of us free-Labourers were compelled to buy our supplies from that store [....] we had a general settlement once each year. We were charged all sorts of high prices for goods because every year we would come out in debt to our employer. Well, at the close of the tenth year he said to some of us with a smile, ' Boys, I'm sorry you're going to leave me. I hope you will do well in your new places, so well that you will be able to pay me the little balances which most of you owe me' I owed $105 according to the book-keeper. But we had understood we had a full settlement at the end of each year. But no one would have dared to dispute a white man's word-Oh no not in those days.

The men had to sign forms of acknowledgement, ostensibly to be allowed to leave, but the next morning they were arrested and taken to the Senator's peon camp to work off the debt in hard labour,

> Really, we had made ourselves lifetime slaves, or peons. But call it slavery, peonage, or what not; the truth is we lived in a hell on earth what time we spent in the Senator's peon camp. [25]

Almost thirty years previously the foresters of Belize had instigated their own' advance and truck' system. Although both had largely similar aims, that of compelling labour to remain in the employ of their former slave masters, Engerman claims that debt peonage in the South existed to make, 'monopoly profits from credit provisions'. [26]

An important part of this process was the rise of merchant capital and towns, which became important commercial centres. Douglas Dowd states that, often, the planter-merchant-creditor were one, but just as often the merchant-creditor was separate from the planter. The latter was just as likely (though not as affected) to be a victim of debt as was the Negro. Foreclosures were frequent and unpublicised, and insurance companies and banks were beginning to take-over some plantations. [27] The South Carolina company of Smith and Melton were making advances of $20,000 annually to Chester farmers alone in agricultural supplies, often receiving payment in cotton. [28] The system was condemned by planters and tenants alike, due to the high cost of credit; between 20% and 50% above the marked goods price in Chester; 40% to 80% per-annum throughout the South. [29] However, within ten years the system had become so entrenched, as revealed by the *Yorkville Enquirer's* apt summary,

> We have serious doubts about abolishing the system [....]. The majority of the labouring classes of the country are today within one month's rations on hand [and] by far the greatest number of those whose business it is to cultivate the soil are utterly unable to make another crop unless they receive assistance from some quarter. [30]

The rise of this new financial capital, though in its infancy in the South, reveals a shift in power from the old planter class, still attempting to recreate their ante-bellum authority to the bankers and Northern industrialists who, according to Dowd were beginning to colonise the South. [31]

Nevertheless, this shift in dominance had little immediate meaning for the Negro, who remained, along with the poor white, an exploited class. As well as high interest rates to contend with, as has been shown, 'Illiterate and. ignorant Negroes had neither the information to recognise or demand honest bookkeeping'. [32] The high cost of guano needed to resuscitate mined soil, bad methods of farming, and fluctuating crop prices kept the Negro and sometimes the planters on a downward spiral of 'rising costs, falling prices increasing indebtedness, poverty, and for the most part, peonage'. [33] However Blacks at the bottom of a chain of exploitation would have to bear most of the weight.

Although the results of indebtedness were similar in Belize, the methods and motives differed slightly. The procedure there depended upon exploiting an annual holiday period. Contracts for foresting were signed just before Christmas and labourers were given, four months advance of wages, supposedly to purchase supplies. However this was the only time the Negro spent with his family and friends before the 'long and arduous and isolated season in the mahogany camps, so they were motivated to spend lavishly on gifts'. [34]

The ex-slaves were granted a month's license to enjoy themselves. Byron Foster cites Captain Henderson's diaries containing a description of the festivities:

> The endurance of the Negroes during the period of their holidays, which usually last a week, is incredible. Few of them are known to take any portion of rest for the whole time; and for the same space, they seldom know an interval of sobriety. It is the single season of relaxation granted to their condition; and that it should be partaken of immoderately may therefore appear not altogether so extraordinary'. [35]

> Pitpan races on the river formed a much more interesting and agreeable feature of the carnival and a prettier aquatic sight cannot be witnessed in any corner of the globe [....] On race days the largest pitpans are manned by crews of from twenty to forty paddlers, appropriately dressed and representing rival mahogany firms. [36]

These African survivals were exploited by the foresters as a means of social control, as they acted as benevolent benefactors of this leisure time. But they were also useful as a means of encouraging indebtedness.

That these were long standing festivals from a period when money wages were not a concern of the Negro also makes them very difficult to avoid. Consequently the Negro began the mahogany season broke. The following extract from Gibbs report of 1883 describes the results of the advance and truck system.

> But by agreement he is bound to take half of his wages in goods from, his employer, who keeps in his store a stock of such goods as his hands require, and of a certain inferior quality--There is an undue advantage on the employers side--the evil of his [the labourer' s] purchasing in the dearest market instead of being allowed to take his money where he lives. [37]

Therefore, the labourer often starts his contract up to five months in debt. Combined with deductions for sickness, fines for petty offences, and having to take the remaining half of his pay in goods the ex-slave usually finished his contract already in debt to his employer and ready for his next Christmas spree.[38]

The Belizean Negro, like his counterpart in the South, found himself and his family on the spiral of debt, compelled to sign a new contract with his employer. As Bolland states, 'Workers and employers become bound together in debt servitude'. [39] Bristowe and Wright's report of 1888 confirmed this state of affairs:

> It is well known that a system has prevailed in the colony unchecked of labourers being kept in debt by their employers for the purpose of receiving a continuance of their labour. Advantage has been taken to keep them in debt by either supplying them with goods or drink for the purpose, and they thus become virtually enslaved for life. [40]

Ford argues that in the South 'the new economic elite owed its power to its control of credit, marketing, and capital in a region catching up with the industrial revolution'. [41] The Negro in the South was no less a debt slave than the Belizeans but his master, although enjoying the benefits of labour control, also began to suffer under the advance system, though not to the extent of the Negro or poor white.

This system of advances was not used effectively in Jamaica where the Negro could shift plantations more easily, or even survive off subsistence plot or family and friends who owned small plots of land in the free-villages created by the Baptists. [42] The Jamaican planter had to resort to another form of control by importing cheap labour, mainly from India. They became known as coolies after the majority group who came mainly from Calcutta, although many were from China.

Labour Control in Belize, Jamaica and the United States of America

Neither the South nor Belize made effective use of immigration as a means of local labour control. In the case of the South, migrants, usually Chinese and European were used only on a small scale. Once tenantry and sharecropping were firmly in place migrant labour was not considered crucial and was soon ended. [43] Although this does show that local planters were prepared for its use.

Belize first attempted to solve its shortages by importing former slaves from Jamaica. The Public Meeting petitioned the Secretary of State for 825 of the 1,800 slaves captured from Havana by the Royal Navy in 1836. A memorandum reveals the dual nature of their procurement; not only for extra workers, but to ensure the tractability of the slaves in situ,

> The introduction of successive cargoes of Africans which have arrived in the settlement [....] will render it more the necessary for the [labour] to conduct themselves with increased activity and attention to enable themselves to obtain employment'. [44]

However, the scheme was not a success. Many died of cholera, five drowned, and two, committed suicide. Of the 357 remaining only 229 were males. The masters found they had greater success in coercing their own free Black population and abandoned the scheme. East Indian immigration did take place as part of the Jamaican scheme, but in Belize they were used to supplement a group who had never been slaves; namely the Mayan Indians on the sugar plantations of Toledo and Corozal. [45]

Unfortunately for labour relations in Jamaica, immigration was considered a necessity. This became the cause of strife between the planter/migrant group and the Negroes, in an attempt to regain rather than retain control over the workforce. But the British Government feared a return to the Atlantic slave conditions, so decided to approve the scheme and control it rather than let the process become a private matter for the planters. This was a compromise between powerful Parliamentary interest groups, the Anti-Slavery

Society and the West India interest. Between 1841 and 1844, the Secretary of State removed all barriers to immigration from Sierra Leone, China, and India. The British Governments attitude is revealed thus:

> I fully and cordially agree with you in the opinion that the highest interest of the Negro requires that the cultivation of sugar should not be abandoned, and that the proprietors of European race should be enabled to maintain their present place in the society, which can only be done by giving them greater command of labour. [46]

So the Colonial Office felt that the best interests of the Negroes were served by keeping the planters on top of society, tightening control over them and bringing in thousands of immigrants of another race to assist in this process. More likely, the Government was concerned with good order, through the maintenance of the status quo.

The Negro reacted differently. Ronald McArthur a plantation worker in Hanover parish had this to say,

> The attorney bring coolies to take their work and bread. They make good house for coolies, but anything good enough for we Black nega. Now coolie is the ruination of Jamaica. Coolie can never work with we; Black people can work round about them; them is the most worthlessest set of people we ever saw; them can't work, and yet attorney give them fine house and a shilling a day for doing nothing; but when we Black people do work them get plenty busing. Now dis is what ruin Jamaica. Send back the coolies them robbers that are brought to this country, and leave the country to us, and give us fair play and regular wages and Jamaica will stand good again.[47]

All this further agitated the Jamaican Negro, so more deserted plantation labour completely, moved from one area to another or went on strike. Jamaican labourers, astute in their understanding of the local economy, easily recognised the damage immigrant labour was doing to their ability to resist their employer's coercive tactics, but many knew the wisdom of conciliation. One Richard Nelstor pointed out to his fellow strikers: 'If no money were made on the estates no one could live, for if a carpenter sells a chair or a table, the man who buys it must get his money from the estate'. [48] Unfortunately the planters had

Labour Control in Belize, Jamaica and the United States of America

grasped the new economics of wage labour less effectively than their own workforce; responding with threats to tighten the vagrancy laws. Some misguided employers publicly stated that it would be more advantageous to be under the American flag in order to 'restore command over labour.'[49] Annexation to a Slave Republic revived memories: 'white and brown people were want to make them slaves again'. [50] It was obviously difficult for the planter to forget that his workers were no longer chattels.

Immigration had stirred up old antagonisms and Jamaican labourers were determined to resist any threats to make them slaves again; de facto or de jure. As the tenth anniversary of final Emancipation approached, the planters fearing insurrection, wanted to call out the militia. Fortunately, the situation was calmed by the Governor's assurances that the worker's freedoms would be jealously guarded. [51] Once again, the Colonial authority was more concerned with quietening the situation while the planters seemed bent on making matters worse.

By the 1860s, when the Indian Government called a halt, 26,000 immigrants had settled in Jamaica according to Knox. However this was against a Negro population in excess of 400,000.[52] Immigration had caused greater labour problems for master and servant than it solved. Europeans had always proved unamenable towards plantation work, and often died from tropical diseases. The Chinese preferred trade and business, whereas East Indians found their new conditions a vast improvement on Calcutta, Madras, and Bombay, but they were never many in numbers until the 1860s.[53] This form of labour control was not a great success for the above reasons. However, additionally planters competed with each other for labour, instead of co-operating as they did on Local Assembly matters.

These freedoms provoked the planters into further vindictive legislation, particularly shifting the burden of taxation to the poor. For instance

Peter Hitchen

by 1865 the excise on sugar and rum had hardly altered, but peasant crops such as coffee had doubled in taxation, while ginger and dyewood quadrupled. Planters livestock wandered at will and damaged Negro crops with impunity, but hags and goats found straying could be shot by local constables. These antagonistic laws did not result in tighter controls but in the Morant Bay Rebellion of 1865, led by Baptist preacher Paul Bogle. A people used to real freedoms beyond the legal sense could not tolerate attempts to put them backwards into slavery. In all three areas Blacks were able to assess the balance of forces ranged against them and accommodate themselves accordingly. Blacks in the South lived in constant fear of the illegal punishment being perpetrated against them by a politically disempowered white community but all appreciated the strengths and weaknesses of their former masters.

Labour Control in Belize, Jamaica and the United States of America

References

1. Sales of Negroes. Estate of P.C.Wall.7 July 1835, CO 318/117.

2. O. Nigel Bolland, *Colonialism and Resistance in Belize: Essays in Historical Sociology*, (Benque Viejo del Carmen, Belize 1988) 96.

3. F. R. Augier et al (eds) *The Making of the West Indies* (Trinidad.1950)188.

4. Douglas F. Dowd, 'Economic Development in West and South', *Journal of Economic History* (1956) 16, 4, 565.

5. Lacey K. Ford, 'Rednecks and Merchants: Economic Development and Social Tensions in the South Carolina Up-Country, 1865-1900', *Journal of American History* (1984) 72, 2, 304.

6. Swithin Wilmot, 'Emancipation in action: Worker's conflict in Jamaica, 1838-1840' (1986) *Jamaica Journal*, 19, 3, 55.

7. Ibid, 56.

8. Abigail Bakan, 'Plantation slavery and the Capitalist mode of production: An analysis of the development of the Jamaican labour force', *Studies in Political Economy* (1987) 22, 93.

9. Swithin Wilmot, 'Emancipation in action: Worker's conflict in Jamaica, 1838-1840' (1986) 57.

10. Enclosed letter of Darling to Smith, 13 May 1839. CO 137/243.

11. James Walker to Superintendent McDonald, 12 Feb 1838. CO 123/52.

12. Alexander MacDonald's report of 8 April 1839. CO 123/55.

13. *New York Times* 2 April 1877 page 2, in Ralph Shlomowitz, 'On Punishments and Rewards in Coercive Labour Systems: Comparative Perspectives' (1991) *Slavery and Abolition*, 12, 2, 98.

14. Ibid.

15. Ibid, 99.

16. Alabama planter cited in C. Vann Woodward, *The Origins of the New South* (Baton Rouge 1951) 39.

17. 'The life story of a Negro peon', in Hamilton Holt, *The Life Stories of Undistinguished Americans: as told by themselves* (London 1990) 117.

18. Alabama Planter cited in C. Vann Woodward, *The Origins of the New South*, 39.

19. Senate Executive Document No. 27, 39 Congress, 1 Session. Statement of General Swayne in Walter Fleming (eds) *Documentary History of Reconstruction* (Massachusetts 1960) 266.

[20.] Jerrell H. Shofner, 'The Black Codes' in N. Huggins et al, *Key Issues in the Afro-American Experience*, Vol. 2 (San Diego 1971) 37.

[21.] Acts and Resolutions of General Assembly of Florida, 1865-66. 12 January 1866, in Walter Fleming (eds) *Documentary History of Reconstruction* (Massachusetts 1960) 32.

[22.] Jerrell H. Shofner, 'The Black Codes' in N. Huggins et al, *Key Issues in the Afro-American Experience*, 38.

[23.] Swithin Wilmot, 'Emancipation in action: Worker's conflict in Jamaica, 1838-1840' (1986) 57-58.

[24.] A. J. G. Knox, 'Opportunities and Opposition: The Rise of Jamaica's Black Peasantry and the Nature of Planter Resistance', *Canadian Review of Sociology and Anthropology* (1977) 14, 4, 392.

[25.] 'The life story of a Negro peon', in Hamilton Holt, *The Life Stories of Undistinguished Americans: as told by themselves*, 119.

[26.] Stanley L. Engerman, 'Economic Changes and Contract Labour in the British Caribbean', *Explorations in Economic History* (1984) 21, 2, 215.

[27.] Douglas F. Dowd, 'Economic Development in West and South' (1956) 566.

[28.] Lacey K. Ford, 'Rednecks and Merchants: Economic Development and Social Tensions in the South Carolina Up-Country, 1865-1900' (1984) 308.

[29.] Lacey K. Ford, 'Rednecks and Merchants: Economic Development and Social Tensions in the South Carolina Up-Country, 1865-1900' (1984) 209, and Douglas F. Dowd, 'Economic Development in West and South' (1956) 566.

[30.] *Yorkville Enquirer*, 10 January 1878, page 2, cited in Lacey K. Ford, 'Rednecks and Merchants: Economic Development and Social Tensions in the South Carolina Up-Country, 1865-1900' (1984) 309.

[31.] Douglas F. Dowd, 'Economic Development in West and South' (1956) 567.

[32.] Ibid, 566.

[33.] Ibid.

[34.] Alexander MacDonald's report of 8 April 1839. CO 123/55.

[35.] Captain Henderson's Diaries, cited in Byron Foster, *The Baymen's Legacy: A Portrait of Belize City* (Benque Viejo del Carmen Belize 1987).

[36.] Ibid.

[37.] A. R. Gibbs, *British Honduras: A Historical and Descriptive Account of the Colony from its Settlement*, 1670. (London 1883) 175-178.

[38.] Ibid.

[39.] O. Nigel Bolland, *Colonialism and Resistance in Belize*, 160.

40. L. W. Bristowe, and P. B. Wright, The Handbook of British Honduras for 1888-1889. (London 1888) 199.

41. Lacey K. Ford, 'Rednecks and Merchants: Economic Development and Social Tensions in the South Carolina Up-Country, 1865-1900' (1984) 318.

42. For a full analysis of the Jamaican free village see, Jean Besson, 'Land Tenures in the Free Villages of Trelawney, Jamaica', *Slavery and Abolition* (1984) 15, 1, 3 - 23.

43. Stanley L. Engerman, 'Economic Changes and Contract Labour in the British Caribbean' (1984) 255.

44. William Gow to Alexander MacDonald, 1 March 1838. CO 123/53.

45. O. Nigel Bolland, *Colonialism and Resistance in Belize: Essays in Historical Sociology*, (Benque Viejo del Carmen Belize 1988) 160.

46. F. R. Augier et al (eds) *The Making of the West Indies*, 201.

47. *Morning Journal*, 6 December 18 cited in Swithin Wilmot, 'Emancipation in action: Worker's conflict in Jamaica, 1838-1840' (1986) 59.

48. Ibid.

49. Ibid, 60.

50. Ibid, 61.

51. Ibid.

52. A. J. G. Knox, 'Opportunities and Opposition: The Rise of Jamaica's Black Peasantry and the Nature of Planter Resistance' (1977) 385.

53. F. R. Augier et al (eds) *The Making of the West Indies*, 198-204.

Peter Hitchen

Peter Hitchen

4
Violence: The Underpinning of Control

Peter Hitchen

The purpose of this chapter is to examine that agency of control, which is often felt necessary by ruling elites as a supplement to the inadequacies of more peaceable forms: Violence. Clearly, this element can be both legal and extra-legal, but here argument will show how each society resorts to levels of violent control based upon its equivalent levels of political and economic domination. For evidence will reveal that Belizean elites enjoyed high levels of both political and economic domination of a legal kind, thus punishments were relatively light, and legal. Whereas Jamaican elites were politically strong but economically fragile, therefore rebellion and striking were always options for the labour force. Consequently, justice, though remaining legal, was swift, harsh, and cruel, the Morant Bay Rebellion typifies this activity. It is in the South that we witness the crossing of the legal line, because the local elites had very little political power between 1865 and 1877, and they perceived a loss to their economic authority from Northern industrialists, merchant creditors, Black enfranchisement and labour freedoms. Therefore, white elites embarked upon a reign of terror over Blacks; but interestingly one that whites saw as 'proper' punishment and correction, not simply mindless violence. Their purpose, as in Belize and Jamaica, was to maintain the order of their society. Crossing the federal legal line was not a problem to the Southerner's conscience.

In considering why violence was considered necessary to control labour, this chapter will look briefly at the failure of paternalism, which in the South was the only remaining peaceable option short of giving full civil and economic rights to Blacks. This is linked with the withdrawal of political rights from the South. Some analysis will be made of the social elements of white society involved in attacks on Negroes. In contrast to this, Belize and Jamaica will be examined to see why they differed from the South.

Antonio Gramsci has claimed that a society's elites will attempt to rule by hegemony, attempting to internalise their values into the lower orders by passing on their modes of thinking, but ultimately they will always resort to force. Initially Southern elites felt that they had imbued the Negro with the ruling white ideologies sufficiently to continue ruling by consent in the form developed under slavery. However, they soon found Blacks had developed such an antipathy towards methods of work under slavery as to resist any attempts to continue in this manner.[1] Thus Blacks might be said to be developing their own ideological supremacy. Genovese suggests that slaves and slaveholders had developed between them a 'seigniorial world' of 'lords and serfs' that had grown because of reciprocal demands. It was to be understood by a dialectic between accommodation and resistance. [2] The following quote from Henry Necaisse, a

Peter Hitchen

former slave of Mississippi appears to support the slave's continuing need for paternalism, or the success of the masters in promoting dependence,

> Dey went and turned us loose, just like a passel of cattle and didn't show us nothin' or give us nothin'. Dey should give each one of us a little farm, let us get out timber and build houses. Dey ought to put a white marster over us to show us, and mak us work, only let us be free 'stead of slaves. [3]

This suggests that he may not have understood the concept of freedom. Alternatively, that he understood very well the need for a transition period rather than being free to struggle in ignorance.

Further to this, Elliot Gorn suggests that many ex-slaves spoke of seeing the ghosts of their former masters and talking to them:

> In my dreams at night I can yet see Marse Hampton [....] when I is by myself hoin' de cotton he talks to me plain [....] en ha ax me iffen I is yit en still a good nigger, en tell me not to be disencouraged. [4]

Simply incorporating this paternalism into Afro-American ghost lore reveals a relationship of fear. The testimony of ex-slave Lewis Clarke makes this clearer:

> I was actually as much afraid of my old master when he was dead as I was when he was alive. I often dreamed of him too, after he was dead and thought he had actually come back again to torment me more. [5]

This relationship was based upon fear and not some good-natured bonhomie; a point misunderstood by the planters as a relationship based upon friendly respect, but one was readily exploited later by the 'night-riders'.

Therefore, who were these perpetrators of violence and more importantly why did they feel such force to be necessary. A Southern white woman and plantation owner's daughter testifies as to where the blame lay:

> For the utter depravity of the Negro was not developed during the period of his slavery .He lacked then the liberty to practice thoroughly all the evils of his degenerate nature. [6]

She continues with a description of her father and his activities:

> He had regained possession of the family estate by this time, a large
> plantation and had it thickly settled with Negro families. [....] About
> this time he joined the Ku Klux Klan, and with one of his neighbours
> set about disciplining the Negroes into a proper understanding of the
> Southern gentleman's idea of their freedom, more especially its
> limitations. [7]

She regarded this as training, ' [....] had passed through the very drastic training
of the Ku Klux Klan after the war'.[8]

The local elites, professional and planter, resented the Negroes exercise of
political power. They feared an attempt to re-adjust the agricultural system.
Evidence in the Columbia Ku Klux Klan trials of 1871 reveals that many of
those community leaders were not just planters but lawyers, merchants,
shopkeepers, school teachers and even ministers of the church, all dedicated to
the Klan aim of 'white supremacy in all walks of life'.[9]

While the wealthier elements of Southern society were unhappy about
acknowledging the new status of freedom for Blacks, the poorer whites pressed
to re-appraise totally their position in society. Previously they could always look
down on the slaves, providing the poor whites with a status that was removed
with Emancipation and which they found galling. For whites in general, their
understanding of Emancipation was limited. Blacks were there to labour for a
white man and his family, and those who conformed were treated kindly by
their former masters.[10] But here paternalism proved a more fragile quality than
was supposed by whites with many Blacks refusing to labour under the wage
system instigated by the Freedman's Bureau. The gang-labour that resulted was
too close to the old servility of slavery, and out of this conflict arose the
sharecropping system.

However, as early as May to August 1865 sixty cases of white assaults
on Blacks were reported. As the *Shreveport News* commented, 'Scarcely a day
passed from the latter end of last week, but some Negroes had been drowned or
killed. This is disgraceful and should receive investigation of the authorities'.[11]

Peter Hitchen

The motives for violence were of apolitical and an economic nature. Most areas of the South had installed a series of 'Black-Codes', similar to the old 'Slave-Codes', and designed to keep Blacks in virtual slavery. Throughout the 1860s, the election of Republicans in formerly Democratic strongholds served to nullify many of these codes. Due to this whites became determined to keep Blacks from the polls by threats, for they realised the Black vote could not be won for the Democrat cause.[12]

Nevertheless much violent activity had an economic purpose. The Freedman's Bureau felt that the Negroes had rights over the land and by 1868 were issuing contract regulations enforcing that right to part of the crop for a living. But this type of insistence appeared after successive poor crops from 1865, and matters were further inflamed when many of the Black-Republican Union Leagues were encouraging their members not to settle for less than half the crop, at a time when the Bureau was struggling to get one-third from the land-owners. Generally the Union Leagues were blamed for much violent activity against white property by Southerners.[13]

Retaliation began here, as in many other Southern areas, through the press, which often represented an anger in the community. The *Yorkville Enquirer* stated that the planters would be 'completely smashed up' within the year if they followed the Bureau's advice. The editor advised farmers to, 'pay no labourer more than his services are worth, to him. Whether or not the wages will remunerate the labourer is not for the employer to determine'. This was different from the Bureau's attitude to the Negro as a 'partner in the year's business'. Unfortunately crop sizes ware not sufficient to exploit the current high price for cotton, and both sides were desperate to ensure that their share of the crop should at least cover the year's expenses.[14]

Although much of the violence that sprang-up in the Reconstruction period was concerned with political control and the arming of the Black militia,[15] much was directly concerned with land control and coercing Blacks to work on the plantations. W. E. B. Dubois states,

> Outrages were committed before the suffrage was conferred upon Blacks; before such a step was even favoured by any considerable number of Northern people. [....] One coloured wife of eighteen was severely beaten because in the last months of her pregnancy she had proven unable to do the task of spinning which was given her. [....] The underlying causes have been obscured by political excess and race hatred.[16]

He goes on to cite the case of a group of Negroes who had left their farms and taken up work on the Atlanta to Charlotte railroad. A gang of disguised men 'came whipped them and drove them back to the farms to work'. [17] Thus most of the documented history of Reconstruction is concerned with political violence as below:

> The beginning of bitterness in our country was the disenfranchisement of the whites; and out of that grew, in a great measure their opposition to this movement of Reconstruction. This coupled with Negro suffrage, was the origin of that difficulty. The white people in our country , are at heart unalterably opposed, in my opinion to Negro suffrage'. [18]

However, the work of Dubois and Herbert Aptheker among others has shown that the above was subservient to retaining white economic control.

Forty three year old Hannah Tutson told of a Klan raid on her home . Though they were in disguise she recognised the main perpetrators. One George McRae said to her, 'We came to dispossess you once before, and you said you did not care if we did whip you'. Tutson testified that,

> There were four men whipping me at once with saddle girths [....] I told Mr. Winn I did not care what they did for me just so I saved my land.[19]

Herbert Aptheker gives further evidence to show that a good deal of Klan violence was concerned with land and labour controls as a means of retaining involuntary servitude for Blacks.[20] During Martial law in York County many

Peter Hitchen

Klan members confessed to having joined as the best way to keep Negroes working on the plantations.[21]

After the 1868 election Congressional Reconstruction developed rapidly, making the control of the workforce more arduous. Property holders emphasised the race element in order to enlist the dissatisfied poor whites, and make it easier to exploit Negro labour.[22] One young farm labourer told a reporter how he had been ordered by his white employer to 'kill a nigger'.[23]

THE INCIDENCE OF VIOLENCE IN CADDO PARISH.

Caddo Homicides, 1865-1884

Year	Whites	Blacks	Unknown	Total	% of Blacks	Rates
1865	2	9	2	13	81.9	59.8
1866	6	11	1	18	64.6	82.8
1867	6	15	5	26	71.5	119.6
1868	5	154	26	185	96.9	851.0
1869	3	12	4	19	80.0	90.4
1870	6	50	10	66	89.3	303.6
1871	5	18	4	27	78.3	124.2
1872	6	33	7	46	84.7	211.6
1873	10	19	3	32	65.6	147.2
1874	12	74	19	105	85.8	483.0
1875	2	18	3	23	90.0	105.8
1876	2	3	1	6	60.0	27.6
1877	1	6	3	10	85.7	37.0
1878	4	21	3	28	84.0	103.6
1879	1	4	0	5	80.0	18.5
1880	1	5	3	9	83.4	33.3
1881	2	7	2	11	77.8	40.7
1882	0	0	2	2	0.0	7.4
1883	2	3	3	8	60.0	29.6
1884	0	4	9	13	100.0	48.1
subtotal	11	50	25	86	82.0	39.6
Total	76	466	110	652	86.0	140.6

Caddo Racial Distribution by Homicides

Race of Victims and Perpetrators	1865-1876	%	1877-1884	%	Number	%
unknown by unknown	44	7.8	20	23.2	64	9.8
unknown by whites	28	4.9	3	3.4	31	4.7
unknown by blacks	13	2.3	2	2.3	15	2.3
whites by unknown	12	2.1	1	1.1	13	2.0
blacks by unknown	66	11.7	3	3.4	69	10.5
whites by whites	41	7.2	9	10.4	50	7.7
whites by blacks	12	2.1	1	1.1	13	2.0
blacks by whites	295	52.1	22	25.5	317	48.6
blacks by blacks	55	9.7	25	29.0	80	12.2
Total	566	99.9	86	99.5	652	99.8

Both tables above show a massive falling-off
of Homicides in Caddo around the time of Southern Redemption particularly the blacks by whites
figure of 295 down to 22.

Many Negroes were driven from the land and had their few possessions destroyed out of a jealousy easily used by the local elites.[24]

So, while political control evaded the whites violence continued. Dubois states that in South Carolina,

> in the nine counties covered by the investigation [....] for six months [....] thirty five men were murdered, 262 men and women were whipped, 101 were burned out and mutilated, and two sex offences against women took place'.

Major Lewis Merrill of the US. army testified that in Caddo Parish Louisiana 'killing a Black man was not thought of as murder by whites and no local grand jury would indict a white for such a murder'. [26]

It becomes clear that across the South, the war for the Union may have been over, but the war about slavery was still being raged by a form of guerrilla tactic. The Southern white coalition were determined to maintain a de-facto slavery. Interestingly the table on the facing page titled 'Caddo Homicides' shows a falling away of violence as political power returns to the parish in 1876; a trend which existed throughout the South, with the problem renewing itself whenever Blacks threatened to regain any political power.[27]

In contrast the British Caribbean does not show similar features of organised illegal violence. Although both areas had a distant government with its own views, and a set of local hierarchies in conflict with them. However, the British Caribbean had not been brought to Emancipation by defeat in war, rather by a strictly legal process through Parliament. Of course the American War of Independence had shown that Acts of Parliament were not always enough, but Jamaica and Belize were less threatening militarily and economically to Britain. As Jamaican whites crucially were outnumbered 100 to one by their former slaves, and were mindful of a strong tradition of missionary supported resistance by Blacks, it was necessary to maintain legal but harsh controls in harmony with the British Government.

Labour Control in Belize, Jamaica and the United States of America

Much of the legal punishment of workers has already been discussed in previous chapters. In Belize no serious confrontations took place until the ex-servicemen's riots of 1919 white status was not threatened nor was there a poor white population of any significance to manipulate. The mahogany lords were able to maintain a paternalistic control of a workforce non-militant by Jamaican standards.[28] Fines and imprisonment were effective over what were usually petty absentee offences. Bolland does not report a major strike until the Regalia Estate dispute on 16 November 1869, only two years before Crown Colony rule was requested. The thirty workers who left work, 'without leave or lawful excuse' were dealt with swiftly. The magistrate, Lucas Howell reports, 'They were, by my advice arrested and tried and I ordered each one of them to pay their employers the sum of two dollars and a further one dollar and fifty cents in costs. [29] Justice was swift and decisive, and as Bolland states, nothing really changed after 1871. [30]

Regarding levels of violence, Jamaica falls midway between the South and Belize, in that legal forms were maintained, as in Belize, but punishments were met with a severity short of death that sometimes matched that of the South. In Jamaica, the Crown authorities were less concerned with Black rights than good order. Governor Sligo sent troops to one strike in august 1834 at 10pm with orders to surprise the ringleaders in bed. They were arrested, tried, and punished with forty lashes each by the following day.[31] This serves to show that although many Blacks saw the Crown representatives as supportive of their cause, the reality was a concern with good order in accordance with British Government policy, and would conflict with any party that was in contradiction of such good order. Although the severity of condemnation was considerably harsher if the conflict came from Blacks.[32]

Similarly the Stipendiary Magistrates in Belize and Jamaica were often praised as supportive of Negro rights when compared to the Local Magistrates;

but in reality they were both subject to political policy; the former from the Crown and the latter from the planters through the local legislative assembly, which they controlled. Stipendiaries were supposedly impartial arbitrators but were praised, 'as they went from estate to estate flogging'. John Gaskell, a Negro on Mt. Sinai estate was given 24 lashes and 14 days hard labour for 'insubordination and trying to instil into his fellow apprentices the same'. [33] Crown justice was harsh but it may have been more lenient than Jamaican planter justice. The Stipendiaries gave out fines and lashings to prevent Blacks going to jail. Once there a Negro would fall into the hands of the local 'Custos', similar to a sheriff in responsibility though including the jails. These 'Custos' belonged to the planter class who would inflict harsher punishments. For instance, Swithin Wilmot says it was illegal to flog women but he cites a case of a pregnant woman being flogged on the treadmill in jail as 'not being untypical'. [34]

As has been examined in previous chapters Jamaican labourers were militant and this is the main reason for the severity of punishments. Lorna E. Simmons claims that dozens of localised riots went unpublicised between 1838-1865. [35] But none were dealt with as harshly as the participants and villagers in the Morant Bay Rebellion of 1865. On Governor Eyre's orders more than 430 men and women were killed, 600 were publicly flogged, and 1000 homes were burned. The Colonial Office held a three month inquiry involving 730 witnesses at 60 separate sittings. In typical civil service understatement, the board of inquiry decided that the death punishments had been 'unnecessarily frequent'; floggings were 'reckless, sometimes barbarous' and burning family homes 'wanton and cruel'. However, the revolt constituted 'planned resistance to lawful authority' and Governor Eyre was praised for his 'Skill, promptitude and vigour'. [36] Once again government authorities had been used to re-establish order by violent action, condoned at the highest levels. No account was taken

Labour Control in Belize, Jamaica and the United States of America

for Blacks already being in a subservient position in society with a need to offer some resistance merely to redress the balance.

Due to long standing economic difficulties the Jamaican Assembly was inadequate to the task of labour control. However due to the mahogany boom Belize was able to control all the spare lands and maintain an ordered workforce. Belize did not witness the kind of labour dispute common in Jamaica until the late 1860s. Thus, Belize progresses from individual effort to strike action, Jamaica begins the Post-Emancipation period with strikes and develops towards a major insurrection in 1865. This helps to explain why violence was more severe in Jamaica than in Belize. It remained legal because the economic elites remained in control of the political system, though largely with the help of the Crown particularly the Army under the Governor.

In the case of the American South, there was a complexity of conflicting hegemonies; the federal government and local state elites, Republican and Democrat organisation, Northern industrialists and the old Southern planters, disenfranchised whites against enfranchised Blacks, What freedoms the federal government would allow did not synchronise with the way the old Southern elites viewed Black freedom, which was minimal. Thus legal means of coercion were considered inadequate, so illegal forms of force and violence were adopted until the redemption in 1877 when the 'Black-Codes' re-emerged and the Negro was put in his place. Southern elite hegemony was never lost it merely crossed the legal line for a period of twelve years, although the actual constitution of the Southern elites may have changed and would be a topic worthy of further research.

Peter Hitchen

References

1. P. Anderson, 'The Testimonies of Antonio Gramsci', *New Left Review* (1976) 100, 5-80.

2. cited in Eugene Genovese, *Roll Jordan Roll: the World the Slaves made* (New York 1976) 126-128.

3. Eugene Genovese, *Roll Jordan Roll: the World the Slaves made*, 126.

4. cited in Elliot J. Gorn, 'Black Spirits: The Ghostlore of Afro-American Slaves', *American Quarterly* (1984) 36, 4, 554.

5. Ibid.

6. 'The life story of a Southern white woman,' in Hamilton Holt, *The Life Stories of Undistinguished Americans: as told by themselves* (London 1990) 213.

7. Ibid.

8. Ibid, 213.

9. Report on the Condition of Affairs in the late Insurrectionary States, cited in J. C. Stagg, 'The Problem of Klan Violence: The South Carolina Up-Country, 1868-1871', *Journal of American Studies* (1974) 8, 3, 309-310.

10. 41st Congress, 2nd Session, House Miscellaneous Documents 154, Pt 1, in Walter Fleming (eds) *Documentary History of Reconstruction* (Massachusetts 1960) 180.

11. *Shreveport News*, December 1865, in Gillies Vandal, 'The Policy of Violence in Caddo Parish, 1865-1884', *Louisiana History* (1991) 32, 1, 170.

12. David H. Donald, 'The Scalawag in Mississippi Reconstruction', *Bobbs Merrill Reprints* (1956) H256, 457.

13. Testimony of a Conservative lawyer in North Carolina, 1867-1871, Ku Klux Klan Report, North Carolina testimony, (1871) in Walter Fleming (eds) *Documentary History of Reconstruction*, 246-251.

Testimony of Josiah Turner, formerly member of the Confederate Congress, (1871) in Ibid.

John Wallace, former member of the Union League and the Lincoln Brotherhood, 1856-1868, in Ibid, 23 et seq.

14. *Yorkville Enquirer*, 16 January 1868, in J. C. Stagg, 'The Problem of Klan Violence: The South Carolina Up-Country, 1868-1871' (1974) 310.

15. 'The life story of a Southern white woman,' in Hamilton Holt, *The Life Stories of Undistinguished Americans: as told by themselves*, 213 et seq.

Labour Control in Belize, Jamaica and the United States of America

Statement of Governor RB Lindsay, Ku Klux Klan Report, Alabama testimony in Walter Fleming (eds) *Documentary History of Reconstruction* (Massachusetts 1960) 180.

16. W. E. B Dubois, *Black Reconstruction in America*, (London 1966) 672.

17. Ibid, 674.

18. J. H. Speed, Supt of Education. Ku Klux Klan Report, Alabama testimony in Walter Fleming (eds) *Documentary History of Reconstruction* (Massachusetts 1960) 326.

19. Ku Klux Klan Report, South Carolina testimonial, page 326 et seq, in H. Aptheker, eds; *A Documentary History of the Negro people in the United States IV* 1933-1945, (New York 1990) 582.

20. Affidavit from John Walker, Gregg County Texas, July 26, 1875. Affidavit from George Underwood, Ben Harris, and Isaiah Fuller, Caddo Parish, La., August 3, 1875. All in Executive Document No 30, 44th Congress, 2nd Session, No.1755, pp166,169, in Walter Fleming (eds) *Documentary History of Reconstruction* (Massachusetts. 1960) 580-586.

21. Cited in *Charleston Daily Courier*, 16 March 1871, in J. C. Stagg, 'The Problem of Klan Violence: The South Carolina Up-Country, 1868-1871' (1974) 315.

22. J. C. Stagg, 'The Problem of Klan Violence: The South Carolina Up-Country, 1868-1871', (1974) 315.

23. *New York Times*, 27 January 1871, in Ibid .

24. J. C. Stagg, 'The Problem of Klan Violence: The South Carolina Up-Country, 1868-1871' (1974) 317.

25. W. E. B Dubois, *Black Reconstruction in America*, 676.

26. 43rd Congress, 2nd Session, House Report 261, pp.175, 366 et seq, in Gillies Vandal, 'The Policy of Violence in Caddo Parish, 1865-1884', (1991) 366 et seq.

27. Ibid, 164.

28. Educational Task Force, *A History of Belize*, (Belize City. 1987) 41.

29. Hamilton to Longden, 17 February 1870, Archives of Belize. Ref.106.

30. Ibid.

31. Swithin Wilmot, 'Not Full Free: The Ex-Slaves; the Apprenticeship System in Jamaica,1834-1838' (1984) *Jamaica Journal*, 17, 3, 4.

33. Ibid, 2-10.

34. J. C. Stagg, 'The Problem of Klan Violence: The South Carolina Up-Country, 1868-1871' (1974) 9.

Peter Hitchen

[35.] Lorna E. Simmons, 'Riots and Disturbances in Jamaica 1838-18651, cited in Michael Craton, 'Continuity not Change: The incidence of unrest among ex-Slaves in the British West Indies, 1838-1876', *Slavery and Abolition* (1988) 9, 2, 154.

[36.] Ibid.

Conclusion

Labour Control in Belize, Jamaica and the United States of America

Evidence has clearly shown that slavery made way for a new form of domination in the areas under study. The ruling-classes, as did many Blacks, understood the interrelationship between land control and labour control. Chapter 2 revealed how only in Jamaica were the old planter-class unable to secure all available lands from the former slaves, and it was here that the highest levels of strikes and revolts occurred. However, Jamaican planters were able to maintain, until 1866, a robust political and legislative power, which meant that the harsh punishments meted out remained within the law. Whereas the weak political power of the Southern planter caused them to resort to illegal methods of force, although to this group the illegality was de jure as they believed the federal authorities in the South to be imposing on their rights.

The systems of labour control were examined in a wide variety of aspects such as the wage-rent system, the advance and truck system, immigration, vagrancy laws, contract, and taxation. Not all were successful but all were tried although the wage-rent arrangement, vagrancy laws, and taxation were the most effective in Jamaica, nothing undermined the militant strength of the Jamaican worker. Nothing worked better in the South and Belize than the system of advances, which incurred debt servitude, and unlike other legal methods were maintained by fraudulent book-keeping and deliberate overcharging of illiterate Negroes.

Although the ending of legal slavery was an important event allowing a slow extension of freedom, this gave the ruling classes the opportunity to secure new forms of domination. Further research should examine the wider issues of social control in civil society for instance the political system and enfranchisement, colonial or federal administration. Finally the ideological role of missionaries in churches and schools in the Caribbean should be re-examined to see if their efforts were beneficial to Negroes or just another method of social control.

Labour resistance to control is an important part of the social dialectic already revealed, particularly in Jamaica, though also in the un-cooperativeness and early movement away from plantation labour of Afro-Americans; the latter having the misfortune to be a minority group unlike the 100:1 ratio of Blacks to whites in Jamaica.

Finally, therefore, the transition in the United States, Belize and Jamaica was not from slavery to freedom but from one system of labour controls to another, a system that maintained a de facto slavery.

Peter Hitchen

Bibliography

Primary Sources

H.Aptheker, eds; *A Documentary History of the Negro people in the United States IV* 1933-1945. (New York 1990).

L. W. Bristowe, and P.B. Wright, The Handbook of British Honduras for 1888-1889. (London. 1888).

Walter Fleming (eds) *Documentary History of Reconstruction* (Massachusetts. 1960).

A. R. Gibbs, *British Honduras: An Historical and Descriptive Account of the Colony from its Settlement*, 1670. (London 1883).

'The life story of a Negro peon', 114-123, in Hamilton Holt, *The Life Stories of Undistinguished Americans: as told by themselves.* (London. 1990).

'The life story of a Southern white woman,' in Hamilton Holt, *The Life Stories of Undistinguished Americans: as told by themselves.* (London. 1990).

Excerpts from the letter books of Howe Peter Browne, 2nd Marquis of Sligo, From the manuscript collection of the National Library of Jamaica-

CO for Colonial Office at the Public Record Office, Kew, London, England.

Archives of Belize at Belmopan, Belize, Central America.

Although not quoted from directly the following was an invaluable source for developing a comparative methodology,

Laird W. Bergard, ' On Comparative History' , *Journal Of Latin American Studies*, 16, 1, 153-156. 1984.

The following were useful for a perspective on the Belize's history,

Sybil Armstrong 'Belize British Honduras', *Contemporary Review*, 232, (1344) 15-20. 1978.

Michael, Cutler-Stone, 'The Afro-Caribbean Presence in Central,' *America* 18, 2-3, 6-42. 1990.

Secondary sources

Books

F. R. Augier et al (eds) *The Making of the West Indies* (Trinidad 1950).

T. A. Bailey, *Probing America's Past Vol 2* (Massachusetts 1973).

G. Beckford, M. Witter, *Small Garden Bitter Weed: The Political Economy of Change and Struggle in Jamaica* (Jamaica 1982).

Labour Control in Belize, Jamaica and the United States of America

O. Nigel Bolland, *Colonialism and Resistance in Belize: Essays in Historical Sociology*, (Benque Viejo del Carmen Belize 1988).

Hugh Brogan, *The Penguin History of the United States* (London 1985).

Albert Castel, *The Presidency of Andrew Johnson* (Lawrence 1979).

Leonard Dinnerstein and Kenneth T. Jackson, *American Vistas. 1607-1877* (Oxford 1987)

W. E. B Dubois, *Black Reconstruction in America* (London 1966).

Educational Task Force, *A History of Belize* (Belize City 1987).

Byron Foster, *The Baymen's Legacy: A Portrait of Belize City* (Benque Viejo del Carmen Belize 1987).

William Green, *British Slave Emancipation: the Sugar Colonies and the great experiment* (Oxford 1976).

Eugene Genovese, *Roll Jordan Roll: the World the Slaves made* (New York 1976).

N. Huggins et al, *Key Issues in the Afro-American Experience*, Vol. 2 (San Diego 1971).

R. A. Humphries, *The Diplomatic History of British Honduras, 1638 – 1901* (London 1961).

Maldwyn Jones, *The Limits of Liberty: American History 1607 - 1980* (Oxford 1983).

Kenneth M. Stampp, *The Era of Reconstruction: America After the Civil War* (London 1965).

C. Vann Woodward, *The Origins of the New South* (Baton Rouge 1951).

Articles

P. Anderson, 'The Testimonies of Antonio Gramsci', *New Left Review* (1976) 100, 5-80.

Abigail Bakan, 'Plantation slavery and the Capitalist mode of production: An analysis of the development of the Jamaican labour force', *Studies In Political Economy* (1987) 22, 93.

Jean Besson, 'Land Tenures in the Free Villages of Trelawney, Jamaica', *Slavery and Abolition* (1984) 15, 1, 3 - 23.

O. Nigel Bolland, 'Labour Control in Post-Abolition Belize,' *Journal of Belizean Affairs* (1979) 9, 21-35.

O. Nigel Bolland, 'Systems of Domination after Slavery,' *Comparative Studies in Society and History* (1981) 23, 4, 591-619.

Peter Hitchen

O. Nigel Bolland, 'Reply to William A. Green's 'The Perils of Comparative History', *Comparative Studies in Society and History* (1984) 26, 1, 120-125.

Michael Craton, 'Continuity not Change: The incidence of unrest among ex-Slaves in the British West Indies, 1838-1876', *Slavery and Abolition* (1988) 9, 2, 144-170.

Pete Daniel, 'The Metamorphosis of Slavery, 1865-1900', *Journal of American History* (1979) 66, 1, 88-99.

David H. Donald, 'The Scalawag in Mississippi Reconstruction', *Bobbs Merrill Reprints* (1956) H256, 456-460.

Douglas F. Dowd, 'Economic Development in West and South', *Journal of Economic History* (1956) 16, 4, 565.

Stanley L. Engerman, 'Economic adjustments to Emancipation in the United States and the British West Indies', *Journal Of Interdisciplinary History* (1982) 13, 2, 191-220.

Stanley L. Engerman, 'Economic Changes and Contract Labour in the British Caribbean', *Explorations in Economic History* (1984) 21, 2, 133-150.

Lacey K. Ford, 'Rednecks and Merchants: Economic Development and Social Tensions in the South Carolina Up-Country,1865-1900', *Journal of American History* (1984) 72, 2, 294-318.

Elliot J. Gorn, 'Black Spirits: The Ghostlore of Afro-American Slaves', *American Quarterly* (1984) 36, 4, 549-565.

William A. Green's 'The Perils of Comparative History', *Comparative Studies in Society and History* (1984) 26, 1, 112-119.

B. W. Higman, 'The Spatial Economy of Jamaican Sugar Plantations', *Journal of Historical Geography* (1987) 13, 1, 17-39.

A. J. G. Knox, 'Opportunities and Opposition: The Rise of Jamaica's Black Peasantry and the Nature of Planter Resistance', *Canadian Review of Sociology and Anthropology* (1977) 14, 4, 381-395.

Ralph Shlomowitz, 'On Punishments and Rewards in Coercive Labour Systems: Comparative Perspectives', *Slavery and Abolition* (1991) 12, 2, 97- 102.

J. C. Stagg, 'The Problem of Klan Violence: The South Carolina Up-Country, 1868-1871', *Journal of American Studies* (1974) 8, 3, 303-318.

Gillies Vandal, 'The Policy of Violence in Caddo Parish,1865-1884', *Louisiana History* (1991) 32, 1, 159-182.

Joe Wilkins, 'Window on Freedom: South Carolina's Response to British West Indian Slave Emancipation', *South Carolina Historical Magazine* (1984) 85, 2, 135-144.

Labour Control in Belize, Jamaica and the United States of America

Swithin Wilmot, 'Not Full Free: The Ex-Slaves; the Apprenticeship System in Jamaica, 1834 -1838' (1984) *Jamaica Journal*, 17, 3, 2-10.

Swithin Wilmot, 'Emancipation in action: Worker's conflict in Jamaica, 1838-1840' (1986) *Jamaica Journal*, 19, 3, 55-62.

** ..

The following primary materials were extracted from the above Secondary sources:

New York Independent Newspaper

Yorkville Enquirer

New York Times

Morning Journal (Jamaica)

Henderson Capt. G. *An Account of the British Settlement of Honduras*, (London. 1809).

Oral testimonies.

Congressinal Speeches on Land Reform.

Ku Klux Klan Investigation. (Additional to Aptheker and Fleming).

Peter Hitchen

Index

Peter Hitchen

View my storefront at

http://people.lulu.com/phitchen8
http://www.freewebs.com/multiculturalism/

www.ingramcontent.com/pod-product-compliance
Lightning Source LLC
Chambersburg PA
CBHW030347290526
45785CB00004B/1639